MOMS & DADS
KIDS & SPORTS

MOMS & DADS
KIDS & SPORTS

◆

PAT McINALLY

Charles Scribner's Sons
New York

Charles Scribner's Sons
Macmillan Publishing Company
866 Third Avenue, New York, NY 10022
Collier Macmillan Canada, Inc.

Library of Congress Cataloging-in-Publication Data
McInally, Pat.
    Moms & dads, kids & sports/Pat McInally.
      p.   cm.
    ISBN 0-684-18965-8
    1. Sports for children—United States. I. Title. II. Title:
  Moms and dads, kids and sports.
GV709.2.M35   1988
796'.01'922—dc19   87-31791
                                   CIP

Macmillan books are available at special discounts for bulk purchases for sales promotions, premiums, fund-raising, or educational use. For details, contact:

      Special Sales Director
      Macmillan Publishing Company
      866 Third Avenue
      New York, NY 10022

10 9 8 7 6 5 4 3 2 1

Printed in the United States of America

Designed by Claudia DePolo

To my mother, Margaret, and my father, John Patrick,
for a lifetime of moments, memories, inspiration, and
love. I thank you and dedicate this book as a tribute to
your guidance and your roles in my life on and off
the field.

Contents

◆

CONTENTS

CONTENTS

CONTENTS

Foreword

◆

by FRED C. ENGH, FOUNDER and PRESIDENT,
NATIONAL YOUTH SPORTS COACHES ASSOCIATION

I'll never forget the day our son Eric, age nine, came home from his baseball game. We were living in Indiana, where the hot weather can get a bit testy in July. I was in the kitchen when Eric walked in the house looking like he'd lost his best friend. I said, "So you lost a tough one today, huh Eric?" He replied, "No dad, we won." I said, "So why are you so down in the dumps?" To which he stated, "When we got to the field today, coach said, 'Okay guys, nobody gets a drink of water until we score a run.'

"We didn't score a run until the fifth inning," Eric continued, "but all the kids were thirsty and mad. It just wasn't any fun even when we won."

I can remember how upset I was and vowed to call his coach saying what a jerk I thought he was to put nine-year-old children through such an unnecessary experience. But like most parents, I shrugged it off saying to myself it's part of his growing-up experience.

Little did I realize that that experience changed my life. You see, my professional experience in youth sports included graduating from college with a degree in physical education, conducting a youth sports program for over five thousand children, being appointed national director of youth sports for the Athletic Institute, and perhaps most important of all, being the father of seven children, all of whom played youth sports. I had gathered a wealth of experience in the world of youth sports and knew after all these years somebody had to begin doing something to eliminate the ills that existed in so many programs. I set out from that day determined to do whatever possible to help youth coaches, parents, and administrators of youth sports programs to begin to look objectively at their roles and try to understand the great impact sports play in the overall development of the twenty million children who participate in America. What I saw was that while by and large youth sports was a positive, wonderful experience for most children, far too often the "Eric stories" are real. Situations where young children in sports are the victims of overzealous coaches who preach win at all costs, or where parents vicariously living out their sports fantasies while driving their children far beyond their capabilities, happen far too often and are much more damaging than we realize.

Let me explain.

Psychologically speaking, between the ages of birth to ten years of age, we develop important self-concepts. We find out who we are, whether people like us, and all the important elements that build our self-esteem. Organized sports can play a key role either positively or negatively.

Perhaps this brief story will illustrate my point.

A mother came up to me after one of our training programs and told me about her eight-year-old son's experience. He came home one day all excited, exclaiming, "Coach said I'm going to play in Saturday's game." This was, of course, after having sat on the bench all season, and Saturday's game was the last of the year. The whole family went to the game all anxious to encourage the boy only to find out that the coach decided not to play him after all. She commented, "I could understand the tears of embarrassment and hurt for not being allowed to play in front of his family as he desperately wanted to. But what was deeply concerning to the family was that it took a child psychologist a week to convince him to come out of his room, that life really was worth living."

The above is just one of hundreds of stories people have told me through the years. For that reason, when Pat McInally told me about his ideas for *Moms & Dads, Kids & Sports*, I was overjoyed. Finally, a reference guide for millions of parents whose sons and daughters play sports now and in the future. Never has there been a greater need for the information Pat has provided in this book, from the dangers of steroids to the importance of parents maintaining a close relationship with their children in sports.

Pat and his family are living proof that sports played under the right objectives is truly one of life's great treasures. I hope you'll heed his advice.

Acknowledgments

◆

My thanks to Mike Hairston and Tim Daley, physical therapists, who guided my column, "Pat Answers for Kids"; to the editors of all the papers who stuck their necks out in its infancy; and to George Blake, friend and inspiration.

Also, my thanks to the doctors, psychologists, physical therapists, trainers, athletes, and coaches who always so freely gave of their time, information, and insight whenever I was in need. And to my original mentor, Kim Wood; to my gifted editor, Robert Stewart; and to my cohort, ally, and agent, David Gibbons.

To the kids, parents, grandparents, and everyone who wrote me—telling stories, discussing problems, asking questions, and seeking ways to improve our children's experiences in sports—I'm grateful.

Finally, thanks, Leslie. *We* completed this together, equal partners, as always.

Pat McInally
September 12, 1987

Introduction

◆

Questions. Since the day I left the crib and started thinking about sports, my parents and I have had them. How can I run faster, jump higher, gain weight, play better, deal with coaches, and make it to the pros? What should be done if I sprain an ankle, pull a muscle, or jam a thumb? How can I avoid knee injuries? Why should I run laps, perform wind sprints, warm up, lift weights, play positions I don't like, or sit on the bench behind somebody I was obviously better than?

During my first season of baseball, I wanted to know why I couldn't slide into bases head first like Pete Rose, throw curveballs like Bob Gibson, or play every inning if I was the best player on my team.

My parents worried more when I declared my desire to play tackle football at age ten. Was it safe? Was there any advantage to playing so rough a sport at such an early age? And are expensive clinics and camps worth the price? And why was I so skinny when I worked out so hard and ate up their income so effectively.

Sound familiar? Well, as I reached my teens I couldn't understand why my coaches forced us to wear short haircuts if we wanted to represent our school and how come we didn't get to drink water during our practices when we could have all we wanted during games when we weren't as thirsty. And when could I start lifting weights to get bigger and stronger?

My parents were still struggling with how skinny I was and whether the steroids some people were suggesting might help, whether I should specialize in one sport or continue playing several, and if I could still get good grades with all the time and energy I was spending on athletics.

In high school I finally figured out that coaches knew some things but they made mistakes, lots of them, and that protecting myself and my goals and finding answers were my responsibilities too. Suddenly I absolutely had to get better; I wanted greatness on the field, and I needed to fill out my tank tops and cutoff shorts when I went to the beach.

I WAS WILLING TO PAY ANY PRICE TO IMPROVE MY PLAY AND MY BODY, BUT STILL UNKNOWN WAS HOW TO DO IT QUICKLY AND SAFELY.

Mom and Dad continued facing new, troubling questions, too, such as: How come my coaches didn't see me as the superstar they saw? Why wasn't I into my studies as much as football, basketball, and the parties after the games? Why was I still so skinny? (My nickname as the starting varsity quarterback when I was a sophomore at six feet and 132 pounds was Stork, though I always claimed it was because I delivered.) My parents were confused as to why no extra weight came even after dedicated eating and weight-lifting.

Amazingly, as I somehow climbed through the college ranks and played more than a decade in the National Football League, we continued questioning things and having a tough time finding satisfactory answers. I suffered through five concussions; a broken leg, collarbone, wrist, rib, foot, hand, toe, and several fingers; and shoulder and knee surgeries. Even with the best medical supervision we struggled to find the safest, most effective ways to prevent and rehabilitate injuries.

I finally gained the weight I had dreamed about for years, and almost immediately had to fight off the extra pounds that kept coming which were suddenly my enemies. I had trouble finding complete satisfaction throughout my twenty-five years of competition.

By the time I began writing my column "Pat Answers for Kids" five years ago, I had had all kinds of experience with an athlete's frustrations. My mom and dad had no trouble providing the anxieties, mistakes, and rewards that parents discover, worry through, and face when their children start playing sports.

The McInally side of things certainly wasn't full enough for a book, so I saw the column as a means to an end. I could help young athletes, their coaches, and their parents while I learned through their letters what concerned them, what their goals were, what help they needed, and where the system was letting them down.

Since the column was syndicated in over one hundred papers within six months, a need for the information was obvious, and the letters piled up quickly. I've got boxes and boxes of them now—thousands of problems, questions from all over the country—and the areas of biggest debate and concern are universal.

Along the way I have gained knowledge and have received tremendous support and assistance from doctors, physical therapists, trainers, psychologists, nutritionists, hospitals, universities, and coaches. It proved to me that people everywhere are passionately interested in helping our youngsters improve their athletic skills with greater safety and better use of their time while having fun and learning valuable lessons from sports that they can use in their personal lives.

Aren't these the things you want for your kids? Performance, safety, fun, and personal growth sound like an excellent combination, don't they?

Well, I've figured out one thing while trying to answer the questions that occurred when I was an athlete and those I faced as a columnist: PARENTS ARE THE KEY TO AN ATHLETE'S EXPERIENCE AND PHYSICAL AND PERSONAL DEVELOPMENT ON AND OFF THE FIELD.

Moms and Dads, your kids absolutely need your help when they play sports—not a neighbor's, an older brother's, a coach's, or a teacher's. While these people can all add something, it's you they *need*. You have to provide the information and the drills they'll seek away from their practices to improve. You have to get them through the frustrations, disappointments, and failures, and keep the successes in perspective. They have to have your support and participation, and all the knowledge, experience, and insight you can dig up for them.

Don't push your responsibilities onto coaches or blame the system for its imperfections. Above all, don't cheat yourselves out of the closeness, the special understanding, the thrills you can share with your kids throughout their sports careers. Your participation will provide some of the greatest opportunities you'll ever have to get to know your children; to help them grow and develop off the field as they improve their physical skills; to aid them in handling the teamwork and learning the dedication and discipline it takes to succeed in anything.

DON'T UNDERESTIMATE YOUR IMPORTANCE. NO COACH CAN REPLACE INTERESTED, INVOLVED, INFORMED PARENTS. THEY WERE NEVER INTENDED TO, AND THE GOOD ONES DON'T WANT TO ANYWAY.

Don't let society get in the way either. Don't worry so much about being accused of being too pushy or overzealous;

don't feel guilty if you start fantasizing that your little boy or girl might someday be the next Walter Payton, Mary Lou Retton, or Larry Bird. I've talked to too many kids and received too many letters from them to miss the fact that the lucky ones have their parents at games, watching and coaching them, taking them out afterwards for something to eat, talking with them, guiding them through troubles and sharing their victories.

Don't feel bad about caring and don't worry about being too involved; feel bad if you're not doing all you can to help them in any way you can think of or they may require.

What can you do? What is your role? *Can* you really make that big a difference?

As you read on you'll find problems you're struggling with now, fears you're facing, worries that may well be right around the corner. There'll be things you've never considered and areas you've never anticipated or prepared yourself to take on. As these crop up you'll begin to grasp the true extent of your responsibilities and opportunities in guiding your children through organized sports.

Physical concerns, such as playing better, preventing and dealing with injuries, and using time and dedication wisely, will be compounded by many tough philosophical stands such as: When did I become pushy instead of concerned? How can I protect my child from unfair, poorly trained, sadistic, or overzealous coaches? How can I stop sports from replacing his studies and help him avoid burnout? How can I help her handle success—its temptations and its ego—or the sometimes devastating frustration and embarrassment of failure?

You're the ones who have to take on all of these things. There'll be confrontations, with questions you'll have to react to intelligently, not just emotionally. That's why reading these pages is important. These are real problems, real life experiences that others have faced. Give yourself this opportunity to learn from them, to be prepared when your decisions, your guidance, could determine success or failure for your kids.

I know it sounds difficult, but believe me it's worth your effort, time, and dedication. After all, you're not just ensuring the best possible experience for your boys and girls and making them better athletes, you are developing relationships that will grow, bloom, and last a lifetime.

Could anything be better or more fulfilling?

1

Your Role

Your role will be so broad, so impossible to define that there's no way you can be prepared for everything. Sometimes you'll be called on to make decisions under the strangest of circumstances that will turn out all wrong, through no real fault of yours.

I'll never forget my first day of practice for tackle football. Unfortunately for me and my fragile ego, my dad was out of town for a few days, and so it fell to my mother to help me dress for that first workout. She didn't know much about football uniforms, and when it came to my hip pads she insisted that I wear them backwards, using the tailbone pad for preferential frontal protection. When I got to practice, the older players took one look at me and started laughing. The coach, although a little embarrassed at my ignorance, came to my rescue, explained things, and sent me off to the restroom to change. I was so flustered that I didn't read the signs carefully enough—only the last three letters of "Women" registered, and I went into the wrong bathroom. In the midst of my alterations, who should walk in but the mother and two sisters of a teammate. They giggled, left, told everyone, and my humiliation seemed to last forever.

I don't know if you'll ever be involved in such a traumatic error, but let me tell you it took years before I ever showed any faith in my mother's judgment again.

As you can see, there'll be some weird moments ahead. With that in mind, I think it's important for you to absorb as much as possible, as quickly as you can, in as many areas as possible. And pray for good luck when you have to guess your way through some dilemma.

While you're doing all of that, you also had better develop your own definition of what you want your role to be throughout your kids' sports adventures. TRY TO PINPOINT YOUR PRIORITIES PRACTICALLY AND PHILOSOPHICALLY; WHAT ARE YOU HOPING YOUR CHILDREN WILL GAIN THROUGH ATHLETICS? YOU WILL NEED THIS FOUNDATION LATER ON WHEN COMPETITION, PRESSURE, AND PERFORMANCE MAKE IT DIFFICULT TO KEEP THE PERSPECTIVE YOU ORIGINALLY INTENDED TO HOLD ON TO.

Naturally you'll want your kids to realize excellent health, superstardom, and great plays. Nothing wrong with that. But you also have to be ready to handle bad coaching, bad luck, game-losing plays, lack of talent, laziness, and injuries. If you add lack of size, coordination, desire, discipline, opportunity, and a million other pitfalls, the potential difficulties awaiting you become almost frightening.

So what can you do? Is there some formula to figure out the best role for protecting, guiding, and assisting your children when they need you most?

The best formula I know is really a simple one, no different from what you would do in any other area of being a good parent: GET INVOLVED, GET INFORMED, AND BE

INTERESTED. Practice with your kids, find out the basic drills for teaching proper fundamentals, and absorb the rules and strategies of each game. Then patiently pass on the information, making sure it is understood and used. Find out what makes a good coach and what drills are too dangerous for kids. See that your son or daughter is receiving fair treatment, is being protected from unnecessary injuries, and is being given the attention and playing time each player needs to improve and have a good time.

Being interested means talking things over with your kids. Listen to their frustrations and share their dreams. Help them get better on the field while they discover the rewards of concentration, hard work, success, and overcoming disappointment.

Sports, like life, are filled with inequities, unfairness, and pain, but solutions can be found, difficulties can be overcome, and terrible circumstances can be improved upon. You'll need sensitivity, knowledge, and dedication, but those are the qualities you're aspiring to possess as parents anyway, right? Just apply them to athletics and, besides the good it will do your kids, you can find inner satisfaction and personal growth too.

There's no question that you're going to make some mistakes along the way but, hey, I've finally forgiven my mom for that first terrible day of football. Don't worry so much about what lies ahead, just find the philosophies you feel most comfortable with, work to ensure their becoming realities, and let your children tell you what they need from you. Believe me, they will if you let them.

OVERINVOLVED?

It's very popular nowadays to accuse parents of over-involvement in their children's sports. We hear of parents "living their lives" through their kids or satisfying their own frustrations and lack of success by pushing their boys and girls to be the stars they never were. Well, I'm tired of these attitudes. They are exaggerated and do nothing but make parents self-conscious and embarrassed about something they should be proud of—their love for their children.

Sure there are parents who go overboard, who sometimes make fools of themselves and even damage their relationships with their kids. But most of the time aren't parents at that ball park or field coaching or watching their boys and girls because of their love for them and because of their interest in their children's lives and dreams?

My mom and dad went to all of my games. When I played poorly my dad always told me so and why. Sometimes he was angry, but I didn't care. You know what my greatest fear and concern was and still is in anything I attempt? That he wouldn't or won't correct me after a bad game or effort. And this is what I've heard from so many kids too. They want their parents to care, to get involved. They'll put up with an occasional blowup as long as they don't receive lack of interest or apathy about their play.

Don't worry so much about being perfect. Don't get frustrated or upset with yourself if you lose your cool every once in a while. It's to be expected of those who deeply care and fully involve themselves in their children's activities.

Along similar lines, don't expect to remain perfectly calm and unemotional while watching them play. Certainly avoid embarrassing outbursts and negative conduct in the stands, but don't feel guilty if you find some difficulty controlling yourself.

10

I don't believe parents can be too involved. The lucky kids are the ones who have moms and dads coaching, scorekeeping, working in the concession stand, or sitting in the bleachers yelling their heads off for their young athletes to play well. Be proud if you're out there. Feel sorry for the kids whose parents can't or won't find the time or make the effort.

MOMS ARE VITAL

Question: I'm a divorced mother of two boys, ages six and eight. I really don't know much about sports, but I want to help my sons as much as possible. Can you help?

Answer: Moms are becoming more and more involved in their children's sports. The tasks once assigned to mothers—taxi service to practices and games, scorekeepers, and snack bar organizers—have been widened to cover a much more involved, far-reaching role. Because there are so many single-parent families now, it's only natural that mothers are working out on the field with their kids and becoming a great influence, and even becoming coaches.

Too many mothers feel they're at a big disadvantage when working with their kids in sports, forgetting that many fathers do not know that much either. There are nonathletic fathers and those who don't have the time or patience, or who lack interest in their children's sports. Still others are overzealous and push their kids too hard, and therefore need to constantly reevaluate their perspective. And some simply aren't good teachers and have trouble discussing and explaining things to youngsters.

It's obvious that someone must fill the void left by such

11

fathers if their kids are going to progress and build a good foundation for higher level competition when they grow up. To place this solely in the hands of the volunteer coach is unfair and inadequate. It's the mothers who must step forward and help kids through the excitement, embarrassment, and confusion of youth sports.

For those worried about their lack of experience in playing or teaching techniques and fundamentals, mothers can read books, attend clinics, watch and listen to knowledgeable coaches. Remember, many great coaches were average or poor players themselves, but they've studied, become good teachers, and learned how to handle players with different personalities and skill levels. Certainly you should know your own kids better than any coach, so you're in a position to help them more than a coach who is responsible for fifteen to twenty individuals with whom he or she is far less intimately involved.

I remember that when I started participating in different sports, my father, although he had been a fine athlete, sought out fellow employees, friends, or anyone else who knew the proper fundamentals to help my development. He found an insurance agent who had quarterbacked in high school and college, and he taught me throwing drills and better footwork; an ex-minor league shortstop showed me how to field and throw properly; and a semi-pro basketball player taught me the secrets of rebounding, dribbling, and shooting.

You can do this, too, and become informed yourself in the process. Find the drills you can do with your children to help them away from practice. They'll need extra work if they want to improve because they won't get enough repetitions and individual coaching in practices and games. Talk to coaches and find out how you can improve your children's fundamentals and understanding of the games they're playing. Don't just sit back and ignore these responsibilities or put them on someone else's shoulders.

Besides the physical skills, players will run into many situations where patient, insightful advice or simply a sympathetic ear will be most important and appreciated. There will always be times when your child will fail, be unfairly benched, or become frustrated. Knowledgeable explanations will be necessary, as well as advice on handling problems with coaches, on making decisions about which sports they're best suited for, and on keeping both success and failure in perspective.

Youth sports are an important part of growing up. Almost every boy and girl gets involved to some degree, and I think you should provide as much knowledge, guidance, and support as possible.

You don't have to become an expert, and you'll probably be surprised at how quickly you can learn and how much help you can give your kids. Kent Hrbek of the Minnesota Twins, an All-Star performer, had a tremendous hitting spree a couple of years ago, and I can remember that he gave all the credit to his mother. It seems that while watching a game she noticed something wrong in his swing, told him about it, and after making a simple adjustment he started hitting the ball better. Whenever I fell into a punting slump I flew my father out to Cincinnati because he knew my style better than anyone else. (By the way, he had never kicked and knew nothing about it until we started punting together on the practice field.)

Start working on learning the basics and practice with your kids as much as possible. Teach them to listen, and listen to them. You can learn enough to make a difference in their athletic careers, and most important, you'll be more involved and closer to them.

UNDERSTANDING YOUR MOTIVATIONS

A conference in Orlando, Florida, designed to help make the youth sports experience safer and more fun, enlightened me in some unusual ways. Although I attended hoping to increase my knowledge of physiology and ways of improving the safety and performance of youngsters, I left with a better idea of how to handle other people and how to improve myself.

Dr. Orv Owens, a counseling psychologist, presented some interesting views of the role of parents and how they can best be handled by a youth sports coach. Perhaps you'll see a little of yourself in his lecture. He divided people into five broad categories, personality traits that motivate individuals to act the way they do. Four of these are fear motivations; the fifth is what we should all aspire to be: love motivated.

The first group, the "fatalists," are dominated by their fear of failure. These individuals are apt to discourage their children from playing sports, and whenever possible avoid responsibility themselves. Creativity scares them, and they generally choose not to try something because that way they can't fail. Dr. Owens explained that a youth coach or leader must take total responsibility for children whose parents fit in this category because they're simply not going to help their kids through the tests of failure, disappointment, and injuries. These parents are usually seldom seen.

The second group are the "exasperators." They have a great fear of loss of position or strength. These parents like to argue because winning a point makes them feel better about themselves. They're usually the first to speak up at a meeting, voicing displeasure or dissatisfaction. The best way for a coach to handle them is to give them some recognition. You'd better open a discussion by asking their opinions, or else they will argue all night long. Give them some recognition, make them feel important, and you'll have them on your side the rest of the season.

The third group, the "appraisers," are generally perfectionists who insist on arguing about little details, rules, and techniques. They'll have many questions, too, but these will concern facts and figures. Give them facts and firm explanations, hand them some rule books, and they'll be all right.

The final group, the "relaters," suffer from a fear of rejection. They worry about others liking them; they want to join things, buy things, and be accepted. They want to be appreciated, and if they're not made fully aware that their efforts are being appreciated, they'll stop coming and withdraw their support in a hurry.

Of course it's possible for parents to fit into several different groups, which can make life even more difficult for a youth coach. Look at these personality traits and determine where you sit right now. Work to eliminate the shortcomings and fears that are hurting your relationships and getting in the way of your children's play and their coach's efforts.

Dr. Owens went on to explain that 95 percent of us fit into one or more of these four categories, while only 5 percent of us have conquered our fears and are love motivated. These are the people who express themselves by working for inner peace, accomplishing what is expected of them, helping others whenever possible, fitting into any group in any way necessary to accomplish things, and dedicating themselves to creative, positive change.

If you'll do these things, you'll be better able to develop good young people, not just athletes. Your kids won't just play well and win, they'll become better human beings too. As you improve, everyone around you will benefit.

CONDUCT IN THE STANDS

Not long ago I went to the basketball game of a twelve-year-old boy whose father is a good friend of mine. As I watched the game I found myself growing angrier and angrier at some of the people around me. While most were there to support the players and I respected their interest and dedication, there were some who were loud and abusive in their criticisms of the youngsters out on the court. I particularly had trouble controlling myself when their thoughtless, rude comments were directed toward my friend's son.

Comments such as, "He always chokes when there's extra pressure," "He can't dribble, so why do they give him the ball," and "He should be on the bench," are all unnecessary, harmful, and simply shouldn't be a part of youth sports.

Let's face it: You never know who might hear you, so these anguished outcries can hurt the feelings of friends and relatives, can damage a young player's confidence if overheard and, quite frankly, can embarrass the people saying or yelling them.

Maybe I'm too idealistic, but I believe young athletes should be praised when they do well, encouraged when they err, and consoled when they make major blunders or lose tough contests.

Through the years I've stood on the sidelines and watched NFL quarterbacks writhe in pain on the field after being injured while the crowds cheer because they were hurt and a substitute would replace them. This conduct is unforgivable, of course, even in professional sports, and I really believe it seeps down to all youth sports.

If loud-mouthed, rude people are going to yell at players, coaches, and officials when the game supposedly is just for fun, then they're being granted licenses for worse conduct when money is on the line and national or world championships are to be decided.

When you're at a game or match, try to be positive—*all the time*. Don't look for shortcomings or grade players' performances on execution. Instead, appreciate their effort and desire. Be there to support the kids—*all of them*. Don't let yourself slip into the bad habit of yelling or even thinking negative things.

If you're making the wonderful effort to be there, reward yourself by enjoying it. Don't frustrate yourself or others around you by saying stupid, inconsiderate things about the young boys and girls (or grown-up men and women, for that matter) who are out there doing the very best they can.

As you watch overzealous coaches and rude, pushy parents in the stands at Pop Warner and Little League games, at youth soccer matches and basketball contests, you begin to wonder if this behavior feeds the fire that flares up in violence at big-game competition levels. Are episodes similar to the worldwide soccer tragedies that have been occurring over the past decade really that far off?

Children observe the abuse hurled at opposing players and umpires by their own parents and coaches. Children are smart. During conversations with them and in their letters they've asked why they're told to show respect to officials when their own coaches and other adults, including parents, yell at umpires on questionable calls, threaten them and, in some cases, wait after games to scream some more at closer range.

I'm a strong believer in parental involvement and in the good that is so prevalent in youth sports. I've played, I've coached, I've officiated, and I've attended countless games over the years. I know that most of the people involved do care about the children. From the volunteer coaches to the parents and friends interested enough and good enough to give their time and support, we have a great array of fine people out there. However, we must endeavor to exclude those who are destroying the integrity and purpose of youth sports.

Next time you're at a game don't laugh at or ignore loud, obnoxious fans sitting near you. Ask them to be quiet. If that doesn't work, ask them to leave. If they still insist on continuing their rude behavior, then ask the official at the game to demand their expulsion from the stands.

If we can begin controlling these harmful incidents on the youth levels, we'll not only improve the opportunity for our children to have a good time but we'll also influence others to act more reasonably at other athletic contests. We'll also remind ourselves of our responsibility as adults, fans, and human beings.

HANDLING OFFICIALS

Question: How come my parents and coaches yell at the umpires and refs but tell us we can't do it?

Answer: I've talked to many kids who are very confused when it comes to officials. They're told by their parents and coaches to respect umpires and referees, that they're figures of authority who should be listened to and handled politely. Then they see adults yelling at these same men and women who they've been told are like teachers or policemen.

Kids also see their moms and dads act this way from the stands, and they're embarrassed. Have you ever thought about what you look like through children's eyes when you're ranting and raving after some questionable call? I can remember watching *The Bad News Bears* and having trouble laughing during many of the scenes because the terrible conduct of some coaches and parents was so well represented and humiliating.

I'm not here to point a finger, but I think a little perspective is needed in this area. There has to be a better approach to teaching young athletes about officiating, not the double standard of conduct that has been accepted up to now. Kids can be taught to respect officials, but the adults around them must live up to the standards being impressed on the youngsters.

Your boys and girls should be made aware, and you must accept, that officials make mistakes, sometimes lots of them, and occasionally intentionally. But bad calls are simply a part of any sport, the same as poor coaching, bad plays, and unlucky bounces. Too many of us focus on the calls that go against our team. But isn't it funny that we seldom, if ever, feel grateful when calls go our way? Do we then say to an umpire, "Hey, thanks, Bud. We sure needed that blown call to win the game"?

If it's considered absurd to congratulate an official for a call that goes your way, why should it be acceptable to yell at that same official when a call goes against you?

Let's all change this behavior. Lead by example. Youth league officials aren't professionals, and they're certainly not getting rich for the time spent. Next time you feel like exploding at one of these amateurs, remember what you look like to your youngster on the field; imagine having a mirror in front of yourself, seeing your silly anger and immature reactions. That should calm you down enough to keep these games and strange calls by officials in perspective. Remind yourself that you're there to cheer your kids on, not to defend them and to distort their views of authority.

19

NO MORE HEROES?

These are tough times for parents who have young athletes. Traditionally, moms and dads have been able to use collegiate and professional stars as role models and heroes for their kids. Through the years athletes had become inspirations, their lives fantasized about and desired, their work habits and skills imitated and revered.

Now, unfortunately, our sports heroes have fallen on hard times. Contract holdouts have shown us that money is the motivating force for many athletes, not the romantic "love of the game" we had always believed. Recruiting scandals, poor grades, and dropouts have dampened the spirit and excitement of attending a favorite college, ruining dreams and reducing an alma mater to a stepping-stone to the pros. Steroids are destroying the health and the integrity of the athletes using them for a competitive edge. Alcohol and drugs are depriving us of too many of our young stars, ending careers and lives with frightening regularity.

What can you do? How can something positive be gained from the athletes our kids worship on the field but are so often disappointed in as human beings? The answer is to be honest. Athletes aren't superhumans. Being gifted physically doesn't make them strong mentally or wise in their decisions or above temptations.

No, athletes aren't perfect. In the past, journalists built the Babe Ruths, the Red Granges, and the Bob Cousys of the world into larger-than-life characters without flaws; superhumans who worked hard, treated everyone with kindness, and had no weaknesses. These were the images we grew up with, but now we're bombarded daily in the media with scandals, disappointing or illegal activities, and athletes suffering through errors in judgment.

This is the real world. But before forsaking our heroes, remember there are many athletes who do live up to and represent the qualities that we'd like all of our athletes to possess. There are good men and women out there who don't use drugs and don't cheat, who give back to their communities and care about their teams, not just their statistics and paychecks. There are Walter Paytons who work harder than others, give to their teammates, inspire them, and break records along the way. There are Reggie Williamses who graduate from Dartmouth a semester early, involve themselves with charities, work with youth, and are proud of being good fathers and husbands. There are Rod Carews who have great, lengthy careers, share their knowledge with those around them, and are good for their sports.

You do have to dig a little harder now. Your job is tougher because children simply are not as naive today, not as ignorant of the pitfalls and evils of our world. But even the negative things—the tragic deaths of Len Bias and Don Rogers, the ruined careers of professional athletes banned for drug habits, the gambling and point-shaving investigations, and the illegal recruitment and nonexistent educations at some universities—can be used to better prepare and protect our youngsters. They must learn from their heroes; we must find truth and inspiration from those we respect and admire. If they learn what to avoid and how to steer clear of failure and self-destruction, then so be it.

Cheating, drugs, greed, and selfishness have always been part of athletics. Big money, big egos, and a worshiping public have always led to some athletes getting away with too much and abusing their privileges. Responsibility, truth, and wisdom have never simply gone with the territory. This does not mean, however, that we should discard athletics or turn our backs on our fallen heroes.

What we need to teach our children are perspective and

truth. Sports can inspire greatness, personal accomplishment, sharing, sacrifice, and discipline. It's up to you to make sure you explain the difference between superstardom on the field and success as a person. Make sure your kids understand that being a responsible citizen is more important than making the Hall of Fame.

Perspective and truth, they're really up to you.

FEAR OF INJURY

Countless letters from parents have told me their children are frightened of being injured when they play sports. It seems that many moms and dads are prepared for this reaction in Little League with baseballs being thrown at them or in football with all the contact, but many are surprised when fear shows up in soccer and other activities.

Soccer and these other sports have become the entry into organized sports to many kids, and there are many traumas to overcome and adjustments to make. Being a part of a team and feeling responsible to play well and help win games is quite difficult; soccer, in particular, being so fast-paced and skill-oriented, leaves many young players feeling incompetent and worthless.

Besides physical fears, your child will probably be nervous, and because he or she hasn't learned how to handle the pressure felt from you, teammates, and those watching the game, fear becomes a natural reaction. Many children have trouble immersing themselves in any new social environment, and youth sports certainly can be difficult arenas in which to grow comfortable. For many kids there are the ever-present and real fears of injury because players will get hurt all around them.

It is not unusual or unjustified for children to become frightened. Making them understand this can go a long way in smoothing their adjustments, allowing greater enjoyment and, in many cases, preventing the discomfort that leads to premature quitting. Be patient and kind during this period of adjustment. Besides teaching the importance of trying to finish something they've started, explain the responsibility they have for their teammates and coach. If a change in personality persists, however, including constant nervousness or unhappiness, it might be better for them to quit before the end of the season. They might be better off waiting awhile.

It's up to you to talk to your children to find out what they want from sports and why. If they want to play despite fears of injury and really enjoy a sport, maybe with time and your support they'll overcome their anxieties, relax, and gain the confidence they need. Take the time to explain that injuries are a part of all sports, not just the particular activity they're involved in, and that if they enjoy playing, they'll have to accept the fact that there will be some pain no matter what the sport.

If it's a particular sport that scares your child, however, then I'd try to find another with which the child would be more comfortable and confident playing. There are plenty of sports to choose from, so don't be limited by the more popular ones. And if your boy or girl is more comfortable outside of group situations, introduce him or her to individual sports such as tennis, golf, or gymnastics.

If your child does not desire to play the same sport again the following year and you persist in encouraging him or her or, even worse, making him or her play, then you've gone too far. It is much better to help your children find activities that they enjoy and then support them. You'll all be a lot happier in the end.

QUITTING

Question: Have you ever almost quit playing football? I'm second string behind someone I know I'm better than, and I want to tell the coach off and quit.

Answer: I can't remember playing in any sport at any level, starting at age eight all the way through high school, college, and the pros, that I didn't want to quit at times, especially when I found myself behind someone I felt I was better than. Part of being a good athlete is believing in yourself, and it's not only natural but almost essential to think you're better than the teammate you're competing against for a starting position.

Quitting should be your child's absolute last resort, however. There are so many factors involved in athletics that can change an intolerable situation into a great opportunity. First of all, as an underclassman, he or she might have to develop some patience and wait a year or two for the chance to play as a starter. During this time the athlete should avoid moping around and must continue working as hard as possible to improve and prepare to play every game.

Think about all the ways an athlete could move ahead of the person in front, and remind him or her of these constantly. Though one shouldn't ever wish it on anyone, a teammate could get injured, which would immediately throw everything on your child's shoulders. A starter could perform poorly, allowing the coach to send in your child as a substitute who could then win the position through superior performance. Perhaps a good attitude in practice and a lack of effort by a first stringer might convince the coach that the position should go to your child.

In all of these cases you should note that only through continued hard work and preparation will your kids really be ready to take advantage of an opportunity when it presents itself. If they happen to be caught behind a great talent, they might sit down with the coach and ask if there is a possibility of another position at which they could contribute immediately. They could always return to their former position if the situation changes. Perhaps they're more valuable as a substitute, as many great players have been through the years. Remember, they're not just playing for themselves and what's best for them; they must also consider what's good for the team.

Another reason to keep playing as long as possible is that they might just get lucky. Steve Bartkowski of the Atlanta Falcons once told me this story. After his junior year at the University of California at Berkeley, he was going to quit because he was tired of competing with Vince Ferragamo, who also later played in the NFL, for the starting quarterback position. Well, evidently so was Vince, who suddenly transferred to Nebraska, leaving the job to Steve. He played his senior year, made All-American, was chosen as the first player in the draft, and made All-Pro many times.

The best advice I can give your children was given to me by my coach at Harvard, Joe Restic. My sophomore year I was on the bench behind someone who in my opinion was considerably less talented, and I got so angry that I went into Coach Restic's office to declare that I was quitting. I thought it was such a threat that he would at least try to talk me into staying or promise to play me more, but he didn't. What he did do made me feel small and unimportant at the time but in the end saved my career. He simply told me to quit if I wanted to but that I was the one who would be the loser; football would go on and he'd still have his job, but I would lose something very important to me.

If a sport means a lot to your children, then I think they should do everything possible to continue playing. But if they'd rather do something else, such as another sport or a different extracurricular activity, then I think they should change their involvement. But before doing anything at all they should consider what they want most and think about the impact their decision will have on their teammates and on their own goals and future athletic endeavors.

TALENTED BUT LAZY ATHLETES

Questions: How would you motivate a young athlete who is gifted but lazy? Won't this catch up with him? Couldn't he be injured if he's not prepared?

Answers: Many parents and coaches have asked me for help in motivating young athletes, particularly gifted ones who appear to be getting by on their natural gifts. They all feel that these boys and girls would be much better if they were more serious, harder working, and more disciplined.

All of us must get serious about whatever it is we have decided to dedicate our energies to. For some it may be a medical career, playing an instrument, or a better job requiring further study or experience. For athletes this change in attitude may occur at any age, not necessarily when it would be most advantageous, and it isn't something that can be forced on them, especially when they're very young.

If you have to face this problem, I wouldn't put extra pressure on children just because they are talented and you see them slacking off. It's enough that kids should have a good time and mature naturally. MANY GREAT ATHLETES SIMPLY ENJOY THE GIFTS THEY'VE BEEN GIVEN, AND PLAYING IS SATISFACTION ENOUGH. IT'S NOT FOR YOU TO DEMAND THAT

YOUR CHILDREN SHOULD REACH BEYOND THIS LEVEL AT ANY GIVEN AGE.

Certainly your support and guidance are critical in your children's development on and off the playing field. But don't make the mistake of pushing them too hard or living through their play. You should explain to young athletes that if sports are important to them, they'll eventually have to be more disciplined or else other athletes with less talent will pass them by. Also, if they wish to play for their high school, earn a college scholarship, or perhaps even sign a professional contract, they'll have to work just as hard as less talented teammates and opponents to stay ahead and outperform their competition.

Concern with the safety of an athlete who is giving less than everything is well based. As he or she plays on higher levels, it will be necessary to lift weights, maintain conditioning, and develop concentration and intensity in order to lessen the occurrence and severity of injuries. Work habits and attitude will have to grow as the competition and demands on the body are heightened. Preparing your child for these factors is important, and you should be aware of and prepared to take on this responsibility.

What you must avoid, however, is trying to make your kids' goals into those you'd have if you possessed their natural talents for athletics. Having great potential is a difficult thing to handle. All too often young athletes, pushed too hard and too early by overzealous coaches or parents, end up burning out and quitting. As long as your child isn't being disruptive to the team by goofing around or not trying, his or her play shouldn't be regarded as less outstanding just because he or she appears to be less "hungry" than others. THERE IS NO CLEARCUT RATIO OF HARD WORK TO PERFORMANCE IN YOUTH SPORTS.

Pushing some kids harder can actually result in poorer

play. Another thing to consider is that some children may be better than those around them because they've matured more quickly. It's not uncommon for great performers on one level to be surpassed when they reach the next level. Your son or daughter may become as dedicated and serious as you'd like later on but be passed up by bigger, faster athletes who were late bloomers or even more dedicated than your child. You must prepare yourself for this possibility because it will be just as crucial for you to comfort your boy or girl when he or she fails to make the grade because of a variety of uncontrollable factors.

That's why it's so important to enjoy your children's success when they have it. If they're having fun, doing well in school, and excelling in sports, be happy. They don't have to be the next Wayne Gretzky, O. J. Simpson, or Michael Jordon at age ten. Concern yourself more with what they do accomplish rather than what you believe they could have accomplished if they had been a little more serious or dedicated.

ON THE BENCH UNFAIRLY

As I mentioned earlier, in my sophomore year at Harvard I was second string behind another receiver who simply was not as good as I was. Everyone on the team could see it—it was obvious when we watched the game films week after week that he wasn't getting the job done—but still they kept him in.

I was going crazy, so I went into my coach's office, talked to him, and we watched the films together. I thought I had him when he admitted the other receiver wasn't playing that well. But then he said, "But he has a better attitude.

All you care about is yourself, and this is a team game. I'd rather have someone on the field who's giving everything he's got for all of us all of the time, even if he isn't as good a player as you are."

I sulked around for a few more weeks before I realized that if I wanted to continue playing football and eventually get on the field during games, I was the one who had to change. I stopped complaining about my situation and started to work on the things my coach had suggested and to concentrate on getting better instead of just begging for the playing time I thought I deserved.

There may be times when you feel your children are getting a raw deal, that they're obviously better than the person they're behind. You'll be angry and want to give the coach a piece of your mind, but prior to doing so, take a little extra time for some objective analysis of the situation. Ask yourself questions such as: Is my son or daughter really as physically capable as the player who's starting? Is my child working hard enough in practices, improving and hustling enough? Is his or her attitude toward teammates and the coach a good one? And most important, is he or she a team player, concerned not only with personal performance but also with what is best for the team?

If the answers are yes, then I believe a mother or father should go in. But before you do, I have some suggestions on the best ways to approach this difficult situation. These ideas come from coaches who have faced unhappy parents defending their children's lack of playing time.

First of all, have your child talk with the coach before you get involved. It's always preferable if a problem can be solved within the team structure. Make sure your boy or girl discusses the situation wisely, seeking guidance and advice from the coach on how he or she can earn more playing time.

If, however, the situation doesn't improve, make an appointment yourself but don't go in on the offensive and back the coach into a corner. Instead, ask what areas your child needs to work on and what the child lacks as a player. Concentrate on finding out what can be done to become a starter rather than just arguing that your kid should be playing. Remember, it's obvious the coach doesn't agree with your opinion or you wouldn't be there talking with him or her.

You should leave with the feeling that something constructive has been accomplished, not with the short-lived satisfaction of blasting your frustrations at the person responsible for your child's not playing.

Also remember that you could do more harm than good if you mishandle this situation, so be careful and concentrate on aiding the cause, not burying your child on the bench forever.

2

Starting Up

When the time comes for your children to begin their sports careers, there will be a lot to take on and overcome for everyone involved. Your presence, influence, and insight will all be critical when they make the transition from watching others play to taking the field themselves.

Your kids will be facing a challenge that is worthy of their apprehension and yours. These things rarely go without a hitch; they'll be nervous, make mistakes, and have moments of fear, frustration, and perhaps embarrassment. Not only do you have to help them through these rough spots, but you can also help prevent some of them from happening.

So many kids have told me how much practicing at home before ever going into their first organized season has helped them. DON'T JUST SEND YOUR BOYS AND GIRLS TO TRYOUTS. SPEND ALL THE TIME NECESSARY TO MAKE SURE THEY CAN PERFORM THE MOST BASIC FUNDAMENTALS AND THAT THEY

31

UNDERSTAND AT LEAST THE PRIMARY RULES AND STRATEGIES
OF THE SPORT THEY'RE BEGINNING.

Many elements of sports that we take for granted prove
difficult for children. There is an adjustment to working
within a team, along with the discipline of practicing, paying
attention, and learning so many things so quickly. Trying to
keep up with teammates who have more experience or
talent can be rough. Also, performing in front of crowds,
handling the pressure, and trying so hard to excel are often
tough hurdles.

Many parents have taken a stand against youth sports,
claiming there's too much pressure and too much emphasis
on winning, and that the environment has become an unhealthy one. To them, practicing at home and playing pickup
games with friends is a better formula. I can't agree with
this thinking. Your kids learn far more than how to drop a
bunt, head a ball, or catch a spiral when they become
involved in youth programs. Performing in a disciplined
atmosphere other than at school, learning to work with
others, and sharing responsibilities are all values found in
sports. Add to these acquiring of the ability to handle
realistic pressure, face failure, and enjoy success and accomplishment, and you've got a worthwhile endeavor.

Prepare yourselves for your children's discomfort and
nervousness. I can remember one youngster who played
his entire first season in soccer without moving more than a
few yards in any direction during games. He literally did
not kick a ball the whole year. Scared and nervous, he was
so worried about failing or getting hurt that he did everything possible to get out of everybody else's way. Well, that
same boy played again the following season, and I couldn't
believe the difference. He was running all over the place,
kicking, blocking shots, scoring goals, and laughing his way
through the games that had previously frightened him so.

There's no definitive age for your kids to st;
organized athletics. In fact, different programs (
or more mental and physical maturity. Don't w
rushing things: If your children want to wait another season, be patient. Let them gain a little more confidence in
themselves and their athletic abilities, and sign them up
the following year.

The one thing definitely to avoid is forcing them to play
against their wishes. Sports can be great for personal development and satisfaction, but if misused they can ruin relationships and, all too often, cause pain and disillusionment.
Instead, use this opportunity to enhance your relationship
with your kids by listening to their desires and showing
them that you really do care about what's most important
to them.

MULTIPLE SPORTS VERSUS SPECIALIZATION

Questions: With the competition so tough nowadays, when
is the right time to specialize? Does it differ from sport to
sport? And can't an athlete playing a variety of sports fall
behind one who works full time on just one?

Answers: I had a friend who was a great three-sport athlete
in high school. He was as talented and as dedicated as
anyone I've ever known. After his sophomore year he gave
up his starting quarterback position. After his junior year
he quit playing basketball, his favorite, even after being
named to numerous all-star teams. He quit these sports so
that he could concentrate on baseball, the sport in which
everyone told him he had the best chance to make it to the
pros. Well, he did have a tremendous senior year, was

drafted by the Los Angeles Dodgers, and everything looked great. He had given up the two sports he loved the most, but he was heading for the big leagues. Unfortunately, after a couple of seasons he was injured by a pitch in a minor league game and never played baseball again.

Stories like these are not uncommon, which is why I advise you to encourage your children to play as many sports as possible, as long as possible, especially those they enjoy most.

There will always be debate between those who favor multiple sports and those who believe specialization is critical to success and making it on the highest levels of competition. I happen to believe a combination of the two is best.

Young athletes should participate in as many sports as possible. First of all, the physical skills and the different fundamentals with which each sport challenges an athlete's body promote the development of coordination, eye-hand control, foot speed, and discipline. Each sport has subtle differences that will provide a broader, more solid foundation of athleticism.

Remember this: Most colleges give scholarships to the best athletes with the greatest potential, not necessarily those who were the stars in high school. And how many times have you heard professional teams say that they were going to draft the best athlete available, regardless of position, when their first round selection came up?

In addition to the physical advantages are the mental challenges of memorizing assignments, learning strategies, and sharing common goals, which give a youngster a greater vision of success and philosophy. The young athlete must think of different ways to attack, different angles, different techniques, all of which help to obtain a better overall understanding of physical performance and mental preparation.

The best time to specialize, to apply all of this and ability to one sport, differs with each indi with each sport. Obviously, those involved in sport such as gymnastics, tennis, or swimming have to dedicate themselves early and intensely. For team sports such as baseball, soccer, basketball, and football, however, patience can be immensely rewarding. I would wait until at least sophomore year in high school, and even at that level I would continue playing at least one other sport. The value of an alternate sport in cross-training, retaining a competitive edge, and furthering physical development should not be underestimated.

Athletes who wait to specialize don't always fall behind others who direct all their energies at an earlier age either. Besides the continued physical and mental development of multiple activities, the ever-present danger of burnout can be avoided. Too many athletes lose their enthusiasm for and love of a sport because they pushed too hard at too early an age or demanded too much of themselves.

Playing different sports is fun. It can eliminate some of the pressure and seriousness of competition. It can also provide opportunities to gain more friendships and work under different coaches who will pass on a wider range of philosophies and expertise.

The greatest reason for waiting to specialize is the simplest of all: Young athletes will be better equipped to make a choice after they have gained experience and have developed physically. Too many kids choose a sport too early and then discover they're too small for the sport or too big or too slow; as a result, they lose enthusiasm and an opportunity to express themselves in another position or in a different sport altogether.

Help your children keep their options open until they're mature enough to make a sound decision on what they want to do and are best suited to accomplish athletically. Don't allow them to fall prey to pushy, self-serving coaches or to a system that will try to pigeonhole them at too early an age.

SOCCER

Soccer is a great introductory sport for youngsters. When you send your boys and girls out on the field, they have the opportunity to make many of the physical and mental adjustments that will be so valuable in their future athletic efforts. The sport puts such emphasis on footwork, coordination, speed, and quickness that they'll accelerate their development athletically while learning to work within a team concept very quickly.

Soccer participation has absolutely exploded over the past decade. The reasons are many: The cost is minimal, both boys and girls can compete evenly, and it allows for a wide range of skills and abilities.

You should want your kids to learn athletic fundamentals and meshing into a team in the least pressurized, most relaxed venue posible. In soccer the push for excellence hasn't been abandoned but the enjoyment element has been miraculously maintained, particularly on the lowest levels of competition.

Another thing to consider is the difficulty in performing the basic skills necessary to effectively participate in a given sport. Football, with its complexity and advanced techniques of blocking and tackling, and baseball, with the hard-to-master fundamentals of throwing, catching, and hitting, are too difficult for many young athletes. They become embarrassed and frustrated, and end up being turned off before they've given them a fair shot. Not so in soccer, however. Almost all boys and girls can take the field on the first day and express themselves without humiliation. The premiums placed on running, kicking the ball, and playing defense pay big dividends for inexperienced athletes. And not only can they participate immediately, they can improve rapidly with good coaching; they can advance their level of play through organized practices as well as work on their own, either with you, their parents, or with some friends.

Soccer can be invaluable in preparing your sons and daughters for other team sports, but don't discount the possibility that they may stay with it all the way. An ever-increasing number of high schools and colleges are fielding soccer teams; more scholarships are being given, and the professional opportunities are proving more and more accessible and lucrative. The days when only those athletes too small or too slow to play the major sports were populating soccer teams are gone. The sport is attracting and retaining great athletes now; it has become big time, with much of the fame, fortune, and glitter that have traditionally been the bastions of football, basketball, and baseball.

BASKETBALL

Question: Is it really advantageous for kids to begin playing on organized basketball teams before their teens? I think just practicing on their own is enough until they're at least in junior high.

Answer: Basketball does demand well-developed individual skills that require endless hours of private practice. However, it also calls for the experience and ability to apply those individual skills within a team concept against competition. Thus, the more your children play in organized settings, the greater they'll gain a "feel" for the game and the better they'll understand how to use the things they've worked on and developed on their own.

Many parents feel that kids can learn enough without playing on a team until they reach junior high school, but many of the subtle advantages to youth basketball go far beyond merely learning to shoot, rebound, and dribble. Having personally coached youngsters ages six to twelve for a number of years, I've watched these kids grow as players and improve at a far faster rate than those who chose to wait until their teens.

Perhaps I can explain why. Although basketball fundamentals appear simple, a number of techniques and strategies are best developed in practices and games, and then perfected on a player's own time. Your kids will learn not only from their coaches but from teammates. They need to try new moves, work on defensive fundamentals, improve rebound positioning, and handle the pressures of game situations; they can then take this knowledge and experience into their own workouts. Leaning zone and man-to-man defenses, passing the ball, setting picks, rolling to the basket, and following missed shots all need to be developed within an organized atmosphere.

I'm also strongly in favor of participating in youth basketball programs because the sport involves many physical elements, such as eye-hand coordination, timing, running, jumping, and foot movement. It's an activity of foot speed, one that youngsters can practice easily either by themselves or with friends. The skills and team-oriented philosophies, the individual work habits, and the sheer excitement of playing make basketball a strong entry-level activity for young athletes.

All of these things and your children's desire to play should be more than enough to convince you that youth basketball is definitely worth the involvement. Make sure to practice with them before tryouts, get them as ready as possible, and then continue encouraging them and working with them on their games. You can help them develop individually while they're absorbing the sport through coaches and teammates. This is a great combination that shouldn't be missed.

TACKLE FOOTBALL

Question: Our son, ten, has begun playing tackle football. I'm wondering if there is really any reason for kids to play such a rough sport at that age. Are there advantages?

Answer: The primary reason for youth tackle football is that kids want to play it. Even with the emergence of wide-spread soccer leagues, participation in football has not diminished. In fact, it's more popular than ever, and leagues for eight- and nine-year-olds have flourished, along with the more traditional competitons for ten- to thirteen-year-olds.

Tackle football worries parents more than any other youth sport. Unfortunately, they compare the sport with the games they see at the high school, college, and professional levels. There are drastic differences, and these make the contact and aggressiveness of youth tackle football far less dangerous.

First of all, strict weight classification is established and controlled throughout the season. Great mismatches in size and strength, which lead to many injuries beginning with junior high school, simply don't exist. This alone doesn't completely eliminate the possibility of being hurt, of course, but it does cut down on the number and seriousness of the injuries that do occur.

It's important for you to realize and accept that injuries are going to occur. Soccer and baseball are dangerous too. In these sports, protective equipment is at a minimum while football players wear pads from their heads to their feet. They also wear mouthpieces, something I believe soccer leagues should begin making mandatory to prevent concussions and lost teeth more effectively.

You may wonder if there are any advantages to beginning tackle football at age ten. A year or two will not make a tremendous impact on your boy's future performance, but for safety's sake there are fundamentals that are best learned when the competitors are of equal size. Learning how to tackle, block, take a hit, and fall down are important in avoiding injuries. The technique can be absorbed only in full, contact participation. Wouldn't you prefer that they occur when your boy is playing against others just as inexperienced and who are close to his size, rather than guys who are three years older, one hundred pounds heavier, and much more seasoned?

I believe that youth tackle football is important in teaching an athlete the intricate strategies and multiple skills so vital to success. This head start will help on the higher levels of competition because the mental aspects of the game are so critical. Also, besides being challenging and exciting, football has elements of teamwork and discipline that no other sport provides. Remember, too, that for many kids their only opportunity to excel or even participate will be on the youth levels. Later, as size, strength, quickness, and speed become primary for performance, many players are eliminated and must choose other sports because they lack these physical attributes.

Youth football may be your children's only chance to

block, tackle, get in a huddle, and jog to the line of scrimmage. I have so many wonderful memories of my four years in the Pop Warner football league. I learned and experienced so many things during that time that I never again felt or shared with teammates in any other sport. Fantasizing about being the professional superstar was great fun. Donning my first uniform, with all the padding and the feel of my helmet, chin strap, and the big number 15 on my jersey will never leave me. I'd hate to see your kids cheated out of all this for the wrong reasons. I say: Let 'em play if they want to.

Tackle Football: At What Age?

Question: At what age do you think kids should start playing organized tackle football?

Answer: I believe age ten is as early as most boys should begin playing tackle football. There are leagues for younger children, some very well run, but I think there are other sports to participate in before age ten, sports that can be preparation for that first season of full-speed football.

Soccer, baseball, gymnastics, and other less contact-oriented sports will get your children ready for football adequately. These will teach fundamentals such as hand-eye coordination, footwork, and handling competition while giving them confidence and time to adjust to an organized, team environment. Also, flag football, pickup games, and just playing catch with friends or parents will help get a child ready to play when he or she is older.

Being patient won't cost kids that much. With good coaching they'll catch up in a hurry with their friends who have played at younger ages. The important thing will be to get themselves as prepared as possible for their first practices and organized workouts. They can find a comfortable stance, start catching and sprinting with the ball under their arm, throwing it if they want to be a quarterback, and work on getting stronger. Pushups, chin-ups, and dips are great exercises because they're safe and will increase strength and endurance, build up muscles, and help protect from injuries on the field.

TEE BALL

Question: What do you think of tee ball? Is it good for boys and girls to play at very young ages? Our son, who is six, wants to play, but we're worried that he isn't ready yet.

Answer: Having spoken to many parents who have gone through tee ball with their kids and having watched lots of games, I'd say tee ball is a great introduction to baseball and organized sports in general. The atmosphere at this level is very relaxed and supportive, not intense or pressure-packed. If your children want to play, let them and encourage them if they're unaware of the program. Physically, learning to hit off the tee will develop a good, level swing that will help them later in youth baseball and beyond. The coaches and parents I've observed in tee ball have truly been there for the kids.

Socially, there are a lot of girls playing on this level, so it's a healthy interaction rarely found in athletics. Participation by all the players is mandatory and well enforced. Scores are kept, but the proper perspective is generally maintained concerning winning and losing.

One final reason for allowing your kids to play tee ball is the joy and excitement they'll experience in wearing their first uniform. Don't underestimate how much six- and seven-year-olds desire to go out and look and play like their heroes on television or their older brothers and sisters. I see no reason to make them wait an extra year or two when tee ball has proven to be such a fun-filled option.

INSIDE YOUTH BASEBALL

A few years back I was invited to speak at the opening day ceremonies of a youth baseball league in southern California. I was skeptical at first and somewhat hesitant to accept, but after the day ended I was thankful that I'd done it.

Too many of us have found it easy to put down parental involvement and their supposed domination of youth baseball. It's easy to say all of these adults are doing it for their own egos or just because their kids are playing, or they're taking out their frustrations and living their lives through their poor little kids. Those of us who are guilty of these feelings are wrong. There are some parents, of course, who are overzealous and distort the meaning of sports, but after that opening day I felt truly moved by the organizers' love for baseball and for the children for whom they were making it possible to play.

I had played on the same field fifteen years before in youth football, and I can still remember how bad it was. The patches of grass were well spaced in those days, and the only level area around had been the parking lot. But on this opening day there were four nicely manicured, well-placed baseball diamonds. The credit belonged not only to the men and women who had toiled in their free time with shovels and hoes but also to sponsors who had donated expensive sod and wood for the fences and so many other items which, with a lot of hard work, had been transformed into a safe, exciting field on which young players could dream and perform.

After the pleasure of seeing the great new playing conditions, I took the time to look at the players' new uniforms. They were beautiful. We forget how excited kids get when they're allowed to put on a uniform that looks just like the ones their heroes wear on TV or at the stadium. As they lined up for team photos I watched the joy in their eyes and the pride on their parents' faces, and I couldn't help smiling. And then I noticed what was perhaps the best reason for having youth baseball: all the family members who were there. Not just mothers and fathers, but brothers, sisters, friends and, my favorite of all, grandparents. It was touching to see these older ladies and gentlemen watching their grandsons and granddaughters playing on nice fields with real uniforms and cheering, so graciously, good and bad plays alike. To them, all the kids were stars, and I loved it.

Young athletes learn valuable lessons in youth sports, and I learned one that opening day. The dedicated people who make baseball possible and exciting by giving the players realistic playing conditions and uniforms are not all self-serving individuals or egomaniacs. The great majority are good people giving of themselves not only to the children but to a sport they love.

I recall when I played, and I'm a little embarrassed about all the things I took for granted: the coaching, the umpires, the ladies in the snack stand who gave us hot dogs when we hit home runs and, most of all, all of my loved ones who came to watch me play. None of these would have been mine to be thankful for without the organizers and committees who have built and perpetuated one of our great traditions—youth baseball.

TRACK AND CROSS-TRAINING

Question: Will running track improve my speed and quickness for other sports?

Answer: As an athlete starts narrowing down the number of sports he or she will participate in, it is important to select those that complement one another. Certainly baseball and football can combine with many, and track, if attacked properly, can improve running ability and increase speed and quickness for many other sports.

A good track coach can improve an athlete's running form, quicken his or her start, lengthen the stride, and increase the stamina necessary to excel in a wide range of athletic activities.

As your children improve their running form, they'll cut out wasted body and arm motions, alter their body lean, and learn to relax instead of tightening up as so many athletes tend to do when they try to outrun someone. Poor running form can be particularly damaging when athletes are carrying a ball under their arm, wearing extra equipment, or trying to harness their speed within the framework of a team and applying it to their specific position.

I think your kids will be amazed at how much their 40-yard dash time will go down once they begin working on their start too. Coming out of the blocks properly will increase their quickness and teach them to explode out of their stance. The first two steps are absolutely critical to all positions in all sports, so it's easy to see how improving this area will enhance the performance of any athlete.

Lengthening the stride is just as important as the start. As athletes accelerate they have to be able to change gears, just as a car does, to reach full speed. Many runners tighten up and shorten their stride after the first 10 yards when, in reality, this is when they should be striding out and reaching as far forward as possible. Making sure to lift the feet and knees, and allowing the legs to extend themselves, will result in a dramatic improvement in speed as distances are increased.

Runing track will also increase stamina. Participants are able to run longer and with greater strength because of their sprint and distance workouts. As their conditioning improves, they'll run with more confidence and speed because fatigue won't affect their muscles or form as they accelerate. In addition to these practical, physical points, track provides other useful gains for an athlete. The intense competition and rigid, individual discipline, so integral to the sport, will help when working out and competing in other sports. Also, running against faster people under good coaching will help improve speed further and increase the ability to perform.

Athletes, even great ones, have to understand and accept that to reach their full potential they have to go outside of their sport. Simply practicing, developing skills, and playing a specific sport is no longer enough. Track, besides being an outstanding sport in its own right, can be very influential in your children's development athletically. You should encourage them to participate in this sport for at least one season. They'll reap benefits that will prove invaluable to them throughout their athletic careers.

LONG-DISTANCE RUNNING

Questions: I'm very involved in distance running, and my two sons, ten and twelve, are becoming more and more interested in competing in 10K (6.2-mile) runs and maybe marathons in the future. They run some with me now. How much running is too much, and do you think they're too young to compete?

Answers: Running is a great activity for all ages and should be a wonderful experience to share with your children. Concern for their health and the effects of competition should be shared by all parents of young athletes, however.

There are definite dangers in allowing or pushing kids to run too far. Too much stress at an early age on bones, muscles, and particularly the knee and ankle joints can lead to some problems that would not only hamper or stop their running but could limit their participation in other sports in the future.

Basically I'd suggest that running fifteen to twenty minutes, four times a week, should be enough. This will build a healthy aerobic base that will help endurance and conditioning for the stop-and-go activities involved in most sports but lessen the likelihood of injury due to overwork. The amount of running should be based on your children's interest level and how much they've been running. Don't allow them to just start running hard, regular workouts without preparing their bodies for the trauma they'll suddenly be facing.

As far as competing in races, they should run only within the limits and the level of tolerance they have achieved in their training. They shouldn't run a few miles and then ask their bodies to take on a 10K, which is three times longer. Make sure they follow the basic routine of any adult

47

runner. Buy them good running shoes and teach them the importance of warming up properly by stretching and cooling down after they are finished. DANGER SIGNS THAT THEY ARE DOING TOO MUCH ARE SORE, SWOLLEN MUSCLES OR JOINTS AND LOSS OF WEIGHT, APPETITE, AND SLEEP. IF ANY OF THESE OCCUR, STOP THEIR RUNNING AND SEE A PHYSICIAN.

If your children are serious about their distance running, you should take the time to explain to them that there are really no great advantages in pushing too hard at an early age. It takes years of graduated training to condition for a marathon, and the mental and physical dedication necessary for success are both extensive and draining. Unlike gymnastics, tennis, or swimming, maturity and excellence come at later ages. As a runner matures, the body and mind become better equipped to handle the difficult load. To push too hard in youth could lead to orthopedic problems and mental burnout.

Most important, your boys and girls should not be running for running's sake alone. They should have fun and enjoy sharing the experience with you if you jog; they should use the training to help their overall conditioning and apply it to other sports. When they get older they can decide whether or not they want to seriously pursue competitive long-distance racing. Setting age group records while endangering their health and athletic future is not worth the momentary glory and recognition.

INDIVIDUAL SPORTS:
TOO MUCH WORK, TOO LITTLE SUCCESS?

Question: My daughter wants to be a gymnast; her best friend dreams of being an ice skater. I don't want to discourage them, but in all likelihood, won't their time, energy, and dedication end in disappointment?

Answer: Whether the sport involves teamwork or individual effort, evaluating its worth shouldn't involve medals or awards. Personal growth and satisfaction should far outweigh these superficial measures of recognition.

Individual sports such as swimming, tennis, ice skating, and gymnastics are tremendously challenging, even though few athletes are capable of ever reaching the top rungs of competition. However, to dismiss these sports simply because of their difficulty would be shortsighted and unfair.

Not everything we do is immediately rewarded or appreciated. How many courses did you take in high school or college that appeared to have absolutely no value to your future goals or endeavors? Yet these classes, in some small way, had an impact on the ultimate direction your life took. Everything we do adds to our experience and our insight.

So it is with sports. Individual activities demand tremendous dedication, discipline, and sacrifice. The physical and mental tests that are involved call upon deep reserves of patience and heart. Don't discount them. Winning medals is great, but there's so much more to be gained through competition and training. Long after the last competition or workout passes from memory, the young athlete will discover things that last a lifetime, values and inner resources that can have positive impact on an individual's life outside of sports.

There's no question that your kids will face a ton of adversity if they pursue their respective sports. Pain, injuries, disappointment, failure, and even despair are all parts of individual sports. Facing tough times alone with no teammates to blame or lean on or call upon during tense competitive moments particularly add up to great challenges and letdowns.

Failure isn't inevitable, but greatness is so elusive that to judge these activities by national prominence or championship is wrong. Instead, concentrate on the personal gains.

The knowledge, work habits, and confidence bred of handling pressure and responsibility, and the ability to overcome less than hoped for performances are all invaluable lessons youngsters can learn from these sports.

There's also the possibility of success. Future Mary Lou Rettons and Peggy Flemings have to start somewhere. Who's to say where the next champion will come from?

The most important thing you can do now is provide your children with every resource within your reach. Give them all the equipment, coaching, and support that you can muster. Watch practices, travel to competitions, help them through the mental anguish and physical pain they'll surely battle.

Don't worry so much that they might be wasting their time. Believe me, if they're willing to continue, to push themselves through day after day of training, they'll be acquiring longer-lasting, far more valuable things than just medals or fame.

Too many parents, in trying to protect their children from ultimate failure, unknowingly discourage and hold them back from going for their dreams. Don't do this. Instead, be there when they need you, help them build confidence in their abilities and potential. And if they fail to make it to the top, make sure they understand and accept that all of the hard work, sweat, and sacrifice were worth the effort.

Don't allow them to measure success with ribbons or trophies, but make them feel proud that they tried, that they went for the gold. Too few do.

FROM INDIVIDUAL TO TEAM SPORTS

Question: Our son, fourteen, is an outstanding tennis player. We've provided him with the best coaching, equipment, and competition possible. He has been very dedicated but is now interested in playing team sports such as baseball and basketball. Do you think he can play these without hurting his development in tennis?

Answer: A particularly difficult and frustrating situation for many parents occurs when a child in whom they've invested tremendous amounts of time, energy, and money developing a skill in an individualized sport decides to forego that activity to participate in team sports such as baseball, basketball, or football. There may be bitterness and feelings of betrayal, and certainly the ego is involved. There are no easy answers other than to handle the change in direction coolly and calmly.

Sit down and discuss what impact other sports will have on the child's potential development. If the child has a great desire to reach the top in a particular sport, then his or her chances will probably be damaged or destroyed by taking up baseball or basketball. Individual sports such as tennis, gymnastics, and swimming require an almost single-mindedness to reach the top levels of competition. Athletes such as Chris Evert, John McEnroe, and Mark Spitz have had to dedicate themselves totally to their respective sport. If your child doesn't possess this drive, then it won't matter how much you try to push: Your child won't make it.

It's possible your kids will simply "burn out" and want to involve themselves in sports that include their friends and will present fresh athletic challenges. If they persist in these desires, I really think you should back whatever sport they want to be involved in and do all you can to help them make the transition into these new activities.

Unfortunately, individual and team-oriented sports are, in many cases, at odds with one another. Specialization has become a necessity in today's highly competitive world of individual athletics. Your children will eventually have to decide which sport they want to dedicate themselves to, and your input and concern for what is best for them will be valuable and appreciated. If you choose to push too hard for what you think is best for them, however, they'll undoubtedly fail and you'll probably damage your relationship.

In helping a child make this decision, find out why he or she wants to leave the individual sport. Is it frustration? Does he or she feel inadequate or just want a change? Make sure to emphasize all the years of dedication already invested and that there are times when all of us feel like giving up or trying something new. But if your child still wants to make the move, then make it with him or her. Listen to your child's dreams even if you're disappointed and don't understand this decision. If you do this, you'll grow closer no matter how spectacular or average your child's career in athletics turns out to be.

FROM TEAM TO INDIVIDUAL SPORTS

Question: Our son, nine years old, is a fine athlete. He's been playing soccer and baseball, but since beginning tennis lessons, it's all he wants to play. Do you think we should push him to remain in team sports, or should we get behind his drive to excel only in tennis?

Answer: Many parents are finding themselves locked into a progressively difficult dilemma. Should they push their kids hard in individual sports such as tennis, swimming, and gymnastics, which require coaching and intense dedication at a very early age, or direct them into team sports such as baseball or soccer, which are less demanding on the youth levels?

I can understanad the concern. Commitment at age nine is a serious thing, and giving up activities in which your children would be sharing memories, personal growth, and athletic development along with their friends is a big sacrifice. On the other hand, if your kids have decided that an individual sport is what they want most, they have made the decision at the right time and will need your support and blessing if they're going to succeed.

It's unfortunate, but to reach his or her goals in something like tennis your child will have to be totally dedicated to his or her racket. Tennis is so competitive and the athletes are so talented and specialize so early that, to compete, youngsters have to direct their training and energies to it alone. Normally I prefer young athletes to play as many different sports as possible before selecting the one or two that will be most important to them. In the case of individual sports, however, this strategy just won't work. If your kids have been involved in some team sports before going for a more individualized activity, they'll at least have plenty of time to go back to soccer or baseball if things don't work out. Having learned the fundamentals, rules, and strategies, they'll be able to pick up these sports again and probably not lose that much ground to other boys or girls their age.

Be assured that if your child has made a mistake, he or she will figure it out in a hurry. Individual sports require a mental toughness, a physical dedication, and a single-mindedness that weed out the borderline talents and desires very quickly. The most important thing you can do is support your child should he or she discover a mistake has been made and now the desire is to return to other sports.

The danger in demanding that a child continue playing team sports as well as an individual activity is that the child may miss the opportunity to reach greatness. Forced to play other sports, the child undoubtedly won't enjoy the experience or perform well, and the wasted time and energy will surely hurt his or her chances in tennis.

If your child wants to go for tennis, swimming, or some other individual sport, I suggest that you support him or her but don't close the door to a return to team sports.

3

Equipment

One of my teammates on the Cincinnati Bengals, Jimmy Breech, once told me a story that really hit home with regard to athletic equipment. It seems that one day while in a sporting goods store he noticed a young mother and her son trying on baseball gloves. After a while, when Jimmy was standing in line to pay for his new tennis racket, up walked the mother and son with a beautiful catcher's mitt. It was much too large for the youngster, so Jimmy asked the lady why she'd picked out such a big glove. She smiled, obviously pleased with her logic, and answered that since he played in the outfield and was having trouble catching fly balls, the biggest glove possible would have to help him improve. She was lucky that Jimmy then took the time to explain to her the error in her thinking and helped pick out a suitable glove for the boy.

Although equipment is generally provided for athletes, there are certain pieces you should seriously consider buying for your children, and you'll need some advice in selecting others. Shoes are particularly important. There are guidelines in making sure the footwear fits properly, and you should understand why different activities call for different athletic shoes.

Some sports require more ankle support while others call for arch support or more padding according to the demands of the sport as well as the position your child is playing. The sole, whether cleats or a rubber pattern, must provide stability and confidence for an athlete while making sharp cuts, sudden stops, and accelerations.

I've included information about some football items (the helmet and the mouthpiece) because these can make a big difference in protection. They must be fitted and worn properly if they are to do their respective jobs.

I know from past experience that moms and dads will do almost anything and sacrifice mightily to buy anything that will protect their kids and help them perform better. Items such as warmup jackets (protecting the throwing arm), shin guards for soccer, good balls to practice with on their own, batting gloves, and even personal aluminum or wooden bats are all provided by knowledgeable, supportive parents.

Take the extra time necessary to acquaint yourselves with the best, most efficient, and fairly priced equipment. It could make a big difference in your children's safety and performance without necessarily costing you a bundle in the process.

BUYING ATHLETIC SHOES

Question: What guidelines would you suggest and what are the important points to look for in selecting the best fitting shoe for athletic use?

Answer: I always knew how important proper shoes were for an athlete, but I really didn't know how to buy my footwear during most of my career. I would amble into a store and just pick out a pair of shoes that seemed comfortable and appeared to fit correctly. This, you'll probably agree, is a pretty weak format for someone who made his living running pass patterns and kicking a football. But I found that many athletes and coaches were using the same primitive criteria in choosing their shoes.

Fortunately, I happened to get my hands on a book, *Sports Health: The Complete Book of Athletic Injuries* by Dr. William Southmayd and Marshall Hoffman (G. P. Putnam's Sons, 1981). One section was written by Dr. Rob Roy McGregor, a leading podiatrist. He specifically outlines eight major points he calls imperatives for a shoe to fit properly. I certainly can't improve on his expertise, so I'll quote from him in full.

1. Heel Height—Running with heels that are too low causes excessive pull on the calf muscles and the Achilles tendon. This can lead to chronic pain in these two structures. Remember, forces up to three times the body weight are activated every time the foot strikes the ground. The legion of limpers are often helped simply by raising the heel height either with heel lifts or new shoes.

2. Heel Cushion—If the heel cushion is too hard, the heel becomes bruised. I call this "jogger's heel," the first socially acceptable foot problem. Conversely, if the heel has too much cushioning, you sink into your shoes and lose some of the rebound energy that accompanies each foot strike. The soft heel cushion leads often to fatigue.

3. Heel stability—The heel counter, at the back of the shoe, encircles and holds the heel in place. It should be stiff to control heel motion. The more it prevents excessive rolling in or out, the better.

4. Wedge Support—The foot needs support against the

rolling in or rolling out of the arch that takes place in running. The best support is achieved by adding a wedge from the heel to the ball area of the shoe.

5. Floor-foot Cushion—Bio-mechanists have proof that the greatest amount of vertical force the foot must absorb is just behind the ball of the foot. To protect the foot, cushioning must be built into the shoe's sole. The reason a person who runs in tennis sneakers feels "burning" in the ball of the foot is that the sneakers do not have much cushioning in that area.

6. Floor-foot Flexibility—The shoe should bend where the foot bends, at the ball. If the shoe is too stiff, it can cause shinsplints, Achilles tendon, tendonitis, or lower leg pain. The stiff sole causes the muscles in the foot and the leg to work excessively.

7. Toe Clearance—To function properly, toes should have clearance both above and straight ahead. You should be able to wiggle your toes easily up and down. If there is extra pressure on the toes from the shoe, irritations like blisters, calluses, corns, or runner's toe (a blood blister under the nail) can form.

8. Comfort—Do not buy a shoe that is not comfortable. You should have the proper configuration at the outset. That does not mean, however, that the shoe cannot become more comfortable.

Since I began following these guidelines, I found my feet hurting less, I've had fewer blisters, and my performances have improved because my feet simply feel better. I'm also sure that the proper fit has helped prevent some injuries such as shinsplints, turned ankles, and bruised heels that had troubled me throughout my career. I found Dr. McGregor's information to be accurate and invaluable, and I'm sure it will help athletes and their parents to select the right shoes for their needs and their feet.

FOOTBALL CLEATS

Question: What type of football shoe would you recommend for my son? There are so many to choose from, and I want to get him the best.

Answer: The most important thing is to find shoes that fit snugly and feels comfortable. Through the years I've worn almost every major brand, and they're all pretty much equal as far as appearance, how long they last, and their gripping ability. The difference has been how they feel, although some companies have been improving models for the special needs of younger athletes.

Recently many players have started wearing the molded, multiply cleated shoes instead of the traditional seven-studded, replaceable cleats that have always been the most popular. This new style is lighter and really grips the grass better, even in wet weather. They're also easier on the feet because the stress is more evenly distributed with so many more cleats absorbing the sharp cuts and constant pounding.

If the field is muddy or slippery, however, the studded cleats might be more effective. If the surface is really bad, it might be necessary to place even longer cleats on the shoes. I'd definitely recommend having at least one pair that allows your children this option, even if they choose to wear the molded cleats most of the time.

Shoe endorsements have become a major source of income for players in all sports including football. The quality among the top shoes is so even that most players wear those that offer the best financial package instead of selecting them because they're better or will improve their performance.

There are many quality name-brand shoes on the market, and although they may be more expensive, they will last longer and perform better in the long run. Stay with these and urge your child to select the pair that feels the best and try to determine which company has made the greatest effort to meet those needs of younger athletes.

THE FOOTBALL HELMET

A football player's helmet is one of the most important pieces of equipment he'll wear, and yet few people know how to select and properly fit it on an individual's head. Many factors determine how effective a helmet will be in protecting against concussions, broken noses and jaws, and skull fractures.

The structural quality of the helmet is essential. The shell should be perfect; no cracks or chips should be ignored. The inner padding involves several options. Some use padding, some use air cells, and others combine the two. The helmet the Cincinnati Bengals primarily wear is a combination of padding and air cells. This headgear can regulate the height, control the movement from earhole to earhole, and provide a secure fit from front to back.

After ensuring the structural integrity and fit, a player should make sure to select correctly the best optional pieces that make up a good helmet. The face mask should fasten to the shell in four (not two) places. A preference for the number of bars may be determined by position and need. A linebacker, for instance, should wear a full mask because of the amount of contact he'll be involved in, while a wide receiver or halfback might select fewer bars to avoid having his eyes be distracted from the ball.

The chin strap should be carefully selected and carefully attached also. Again, four fasteners are better than two because they'll provide greater stability and a better fit.

Padded chin cups can add protection in preventing cuts and bruises. Remember this: No player should ever take even one snap in practice or a game without his chin strap securely fastened—the danger of injury is too great.

The inner ear pads are the most overlooked part when properly fitting a helmet. They come in several sizes, from thin to thick, and should be chosen by their effectiveness in holding the jaws firmly against the pad. These pads are crucial in securing the helmet and should prevent it from twisting sideways. Don't use small pads just because they don't rub and make the helmet easier to put on and take off. This will only leave a player more vulnerable to injury.

If you're not satisfied with your child's equipment, I suggest you go out and buy a helmet. These range from $50 to over $100 and are a worthwhile investment. Riddell produces about 80 percent of the helmets in use, but other companies also have models. Be sure to read the warnings on the headgear, however, because there are many liability cases pending in the courts right now.

One final item: Intelligent care of a helmet is important. Players shouldn't sit on it; this can weaken the various parts and lead to unnecessary problems. Also make sure the helmet is checked before any workout involving contact. The face mask should be secure, the chin strap properly fastened, and the ear pads placed for a tight, firm fit. And the shell of the helmet should always be checked for cracks or structural damage.

MOUTHPIECES

Question: I watch lots of pro football on TV, and it seems that few players wear mouthpieces. Why do we have to in the Pop Warner football league?

Answer: Wearing a mouthpiece is one of those instances when youngsters definitely shouldn't copy what they see pros or adults do. Mouthpieces should be worn—and many players do wear them—in professional football. But even if none of them did, a young athlete should anyway.

Mouthpieces are a little uncomfortable and don't score many points with the cheerleaders on the sidelines, but they are an important piece of every football player's protective equipment. They can prevent teeth from being knocked out, stop a player from biting off his tongue, and in some instances save him from a dangerous concussion.

I learned my lesson several years ago in a game against the Houston Oilers. I somehow lost my mouthpiece but went on playing without it. I ran a slant pattern, Kenny Anderson threw the ball too high, and as I jumped up for it an Oiler helmet crashed into my unprotected mouth. My teeth cut deeply into my tongue, almost all the way through, and I was lucky that the doctors were able to stitch it back up. My teeth were loosened and really should have been knocked out. After that day I never went out on the field without a mouthpiece.

There are penalties for not wearing a mouthpiece on all levels of football, up to the NFL. The officials probably figure that pros are old and smart enough to make some safety decisions on their own, but many have not lived up to this responsibility. Tell your children to be smart, that wearing a mouthpiece for every play, in games and in practice, will save them from unnecessary injuries. Not wearing one will not make them tougher or better, just more likely to miss some playing time and perhaps a few teeth.

4

Coaching

Undoubtedly the most heated area of argument, misunder-
standing, and dissatisfaction in youth sports is the quality of
coaching that children are receiving. Parents complain of
"winning at all costs" mentalities damaging the young athletes, unqualified coaches teaching unsafe techniques and
improper fundamentals, and treatment ranging from insen-
sitive all the way to sadistic.

THERE IS NO QUESTION THAT MANY YOUTH COACHES ARE
LACKING IN KNOWLEDGE, EXPERIENCE, AND PERSPECTIVE. BUT
THE SYSTEM IS BUILT ON VOLUNTEERS, AND IT'S DIFFICULT
ENOUGH JUST FINDING ADULTS WILLING TO DONATE THEIR
TIME AND ENERGIES AT ALL, LET ALONE TRYING TO SELECT
HIGH-QUALITY, INSIGHTFUL COACHES.

The problem certainly isn't going to disappear overnight,
but there is a program that is attacking the shortcomings of
volunteer coaches and helping to guide them through training, supervision, and information. Over the past three years

I've become acquainted with Fred Engh, founder and chief executive officer of the National Youth Sports Coaches Association (NYSCA). Fred's enthusiasm, dedication, and persistence convinced me to read the literature he sent me, which led to my attendance at NYSCA's national convention in Florida. There I had the opportunity to listen to speakers in fields ranging from sports medicine to child psychology to legal questions.

I saw firsthand how NYSCA prepares and certifies area recreational leaders and volunteer coaches. The association is spreading, and all concerned parents, recreation professionals, and coaches should take advantage of its program.

Here are some specific questions and answers on NYSCA's history, goals, and the impact it has had thus far:

What is NYSCA? The National Youth Sports Coaches Association was founded in 1980 in cooperation with the National Recreation and Park Association and incorporated as a non-profit association.

What is the purpose of NYSCA? The goals and objectives of NYSCA are to help children have a positive, fun experience in youth sports. The method used in training coaches, parents, officials, and league administrators to have a clear understanding of the purpose of youth sports and its significant impact on a child.

How successful has the program been? To date there are over six hundred chapters of NYSCA nationwide in forty-three states. All branches of the U.S. Armed Forces youth programs have implemented NYSCA chapters. The state recreation associations of Georgia, Arizona, South Dakota, and South Carolina have developed a system to initiate NYSCA chapters in cities throughout their respective states. Since its inception in 1980, close to eighty thousand coaches have been certified under NYSCA's national certification program.

A particularly effective and important part of the National Youth Sports Coaches Association is its "Code of Ethics Pledge":

> I will place the emotional and physical well-being of my players ahead of any personal desire to win.
>
> I will remember to treat each player as an individual, remembering the large spread of emotional and physical development for the same age group.
>
> I will do my very best to provide a safe situation for my players.
>
> I promise to review and practice the necessary first-aid principles needed to treat injuries of my players.
>
> I will do my best to organize practices that are fun and challenging for all my players.
>
> I will lead, by example, in demonstrating fair play and sportsmanship to all my players.
>
> I will ensure that I am knowledgeable in the rules of each sport that I coach and that I will teach these rules to my players.
>
> I will use those coaching techniques appropriate for each of the skills that I teach.
>
> I will remember that I am a youth coach, and that the game is for children and not adults.

I believe strongly in this program and the people in it. If your local league doesn't have access to NYSCA training and certification, you should pursue it immediately. Children need to have the best coaching possible, and the coaches need all the help they can get.

Take a few minutes now to reread the "Code of Ethics Pledge." I think the points will help you as parents to keep your children's sports in perspective too. These are the things you should make sure your kids' coaches are implementing and the guidelines you should follow in remaining a loving, concerned parent, not a pushy, overinvolved fan.

Besides the NYSCA there are other groups that have experience, resources, and programs that may prove valuable in finding the answers to your questions involving perspective, coaching, training, and injuries. Two of these are:

> American Coaching Effectiveness Program
> (ACEP)
> Box 5076
> Champaign, IL 61820
> (217) 351-5076

> Coaching Association of Canada
> 333 River Rd.
> Ottawa, Ontario, Canada, K1L8H9

To reach the NYSCA you can write or call:

> National Youth Sports Coaches Association
> 2611 Old Okeechobee Road
> West Palm Beach, FL 33409
> (305) 684-1141

COACHING YOUR OWN KIDS

Through the years fathers coaching sons or daughters has caused more arguments, problems, and worries than almost any other area of youth sports. Naturally it frequently happens that volunteer coaches include large numbers of parents who are willing to spend much time and energy on the practice field because their son or daughter is involved. Although some simply love the sport they're teaching, most of the time you'll find the coaches are close to someone on the team.

What are the advantages and disadvantages to coaching your own kids? I've spent a great deal of time speaking with fathers who have done it and others who regretted having

missed the experience. First of all, if you're
able, like a sport, and enjoy kids, why shouldn'
Why cheat not only your own child but also ot
of your talent and enthusiasm? There surely a.. .....
fathers who play untalented offspring or try to make them
stars at the expense of other players—but that doesn't
mean you have to indulge in them, does it?

If you have the ability to help kids develop as athletes,
teaching them the basic skills and fundamentals of a sport,
then you *should* be out there doing it. Good coaches are
too hard to find on all levels of sports. Besides just teaching
the game you'll also have a chance to instill the values and
lessons you should most want your children to gain from
athletics. You'll be in a position to make sure winning and
losing are kept in perspective. You can ensure that every
player has an opportunity to play, improve, and have a
good time. The personal growth and physical development
of many youngsters will be both your responsibility and
your good fortune.

Think of some of the by-products too. Obviously you'll
be spending a great deal of time with your child, not
only on the field but while driving to and from practices
and games, and at home, dreaming and plotting strategies
together. Additionally you'll get to know his or her friends
even better because you'll be coaching them and having
get-togethers after games. Knowing your kids' friends can
only make you closer to your own children, and I think you'll
find that they'll enjoy sharing you with their friends too.

There are definitely things on the negative side that you
must consider. As a coach you won't be able to sit in the
stands and just enjoy watching your children play. This was
one great regret expressed by the father-coaches. Your
relationships with other fathers will also be affected; some
will put pressures on you, and you won't be able to sit in
the stands and cheer on one another's kids. Many parents

MOMS & DADS • KIDS & SPORTS

become lifelong friends and share many special never-forgotten moments together watching their children play youth sports.

One, other concern should be your attitude and actions toward your child, and your child's toward you. Some fathers do not enjoy the dilemma of being too hard or easy on their child as a player. It is difficult to be objective and treat your child as just another player. It's also true that many kids have difficulty with the peer pressure they feel from their friends when their father is the coach.

Despite these factors, if you're qualified and your child's personality can handle it, you should coach him or her if you can. To those who do not know enough to coach, you should get involved in some other way. Whether it's as a fund raiser, car pool driver, or scorekeeper, throw yourself into your child's athletic experience.

There are many boys and girls who don't have parents or whose moms and dads don't have the time or desire to watch them play. Your enthusiasm and interest can be very meaningful and important to them. You are therefore involving yourself not only with your own child but with other children too.

Youth sports can be very influential in the development of any boy or girl. You'll never again have a better opportunity to share in your child's athletics, so I would strongly advise you to enjoy yourself and do whatever you can to be a part of it. Your memories together can be irreplaceable.

WOMEN COACHES

Question: Do you think mothers should coach boys' youth sports? We have one in our league, and I don't want my son playing for her.

Answer: I definitely believe women can and should coach young boys and girls. It's happening more often around the country and is a very welcome movement in my opinion. There are many women who know just as much or more than many men coaching baseball, youth soccer, and so forth. Like everything else in life, it's the individual that matters, not the sex, nationality, or race. I have watched both men and women coach, and in some ways the women had greater patience and understanding, and communicated better with their young players, than the men.

Remember, sports are supposed to teach our kids much more than just how to hit, kick, or tackle. A chauvinistic attitude toward women coaches is close-minded and potentially damaging to children. They'll be working and living along with females the rest of their lives, and they will find women in positions of authority because they are talented and knowledgeable.

Instead of bucking a qualified mother coaching, if I were you I'd back her and encourage others. Our children can use as many good coaches as we can find, and to limit coaching to men only is both a waste of over half of our valuable human resources and socially retarding for kids if mishandled.

TOUGH COACHES

Question: My son, who's fourteen, plays for a very tough basketball coach, and I'm worried. He works the players very hard, yelling at them constantly and always demanding better effort and performance. Even though the players, including my son, respect him in his winning results, I'm concerned. Could he be too hard on the kids?

Answer: Several of the more important issues in today's amateur sports concern how tough a coach should be and how well today's athletes will react to and handle a disciplined and demanding structure.

First, any coach who is a sadist, screams unnecessarily, works players to a point of endangering their health, pushes the athletes without regard to their development both academically and personally, or who is unfair and concerned only with winning should *not* be coaching, period.

But being tough doesn't necessarily have to mean that a coach is unreasonable, abusive, or bad for athletes. In 1980 my football team, the Cincinnati Bengals, hired Forrest Gregg as the new head coach. I can remember thinking to myself, "Oh, no. Here comes Mr. Tough Guy who believes in coaching like Vince Lombardi. He's going to make us do a bunch of stupid exercises, run us to death, and treat us like a group of dumb jocks."

When I told my father my worries, he stated firmly that I was wrong and that I would like and respect Forrest Gregg more than any coach I'd ever had.

How right he was. Although Forrest was very demanding, disciplined, and tough, he was also extremely fair, pushed us to become better players, led us to the Super Bowl in 1981, and made playing football harder but more enjoyable because he turned us into winners and gave us confidence in ourselves and in one another.

I think many of you would be surprised at how much kids today enjoy working in a disciplined structure. They're thankful for the firm hand and the genuine respect they can feel for an authority figure who has earned their trust and admiration. You really shouldn't be so surprised; just think back to that teacher or boss had who was tough and fair with you. Didn't he or she make you want to work harder and ultimately make you thankful because you became better? Weren't those demanding standards eventually a challenge that you took pride in achieving?

Well, kids are no different today. Sure, they'll take the

easy road if allowed, but most of them would prefer tough, firm leadership. They, too, want things to believe in, coaches to instill personal pride, someone to challenge their potential. Don't worry if your child appears to be under the control of one who seems to be too tough a mentor.

Many professional, collegiate, prep, and young athletes have admitted how overwhelmingly thankful they are for their toughest, most demanding coaches. Discipline, structure, and challenge are three of the best things your children can take from sports. If a coach instills these, he or she has done the job well, and your kids will be grateful for the experience.

THE VALUE OF INSTRUCTIONAL CAMPS

Questions: Do you feel that it's worth sending kids to all of these sports camps available nowadays? Will they really learn enough? Are they worth the money, and do the stars really teach the kids that much?

Answers: Sports camps can prove to be invaluable to athletes for many reasons. They expose players to different coaching philosophies, advanced techniques, and fundamentals, as well as giving them a chance to see star professionals up close which can be immensely educational and inspiring. The participants also have an opportunity to compete against athletes outside their own areas and to measure their own abilities against a higher level of competition.

Being instructed by different coaches is very important. No matter how good your kids' local coach might be, he or she will still have greater strengths in certain facets of a game. This might be rebounding in basketball, fielding in baseball, or blocking in football. At a camp, an athlete might encounter instructors who specialize in jump shooting, hitting, or pass receiving—all skills that can help immeasurably in their development in a sport. Additionally, within differing philosophies an athlete can experience new strategies, approaches to attacking defenses, or helping in team defensive play. The more experienced coaching the better, I believe.

I've attended several camps, and the presence of professional superstars is great. The opportunity for kids to meet, watch, and get to know their heroes can make a big difference—not only because of what the pros can teach youngsters on the field but because of the messages they can pass on to our impressionable youth. With all of the negative publicity surrounding athletes, it's good for athletes who are *anti-drug*, who are *reponsible* about their task as role models, and who want to *give* something back to the system that has been so good to them to have an opportunity to express themselves in a personalized environment. Also, don't discount the impact of watching greatness at close range; young athletes are awed at first and then begin dreaming and working on performing some of the magic they've been absorbing at close hand.

Competing against athletes from different areas is also interesting and challenging. Learning to elevate their game as they take on tougher, more talented competition is a big part of athletes' gaining confidence and reaching full potential. We all need to be pushed to improve, and playing against someone taller, faster, stronger, or hungrier can go a long way in motivating a lackadaisical attitude or eliminating a false sense of cockiness. Don't forget, either, that outplaying athletes with big reputations can serve as a tremendous confidence builder.

It's important to realize that the quality of camps covers a broad range. Sometimes they can be measured by the fame of the coaches and athletes who are participating, but this isn't always so. Your kids might learn more from a less expensive local clinic with lesser known athletes and coaches who are just as knowledgeable and perhaps a little more determined to give personalized instruction. The truest measure is to ask participants in previous years. Talk to other parents who have sent their children to a particular camp, after you've narrowed down your choices according to your financial position, geographic location, and the instructors.

It's difficult to measure a dollar investment with what your child absorbs from a camp experience. Everything is so individual: what your child's specific needs are, how dedicated he or she is, and how much potential there is to improve upon. College scouts attend some of the more prestigious camps, and this exposure plus their improvement and performance has led to many athletes receiving scholarships. Also, the advanced skills and confidence carried from a good camp can be enough to push borderline athletes into positions where they may be recruited at some level of collegiate play. For some parents, therefore, there can be a legitimate return on investment.

This, however, isn't the major concern of most moms and dads. Rather, the motivations that lead parents to send young athletes to camps are a desire to give their kids the greatest chance for success and to reach their best; to give them the tools and experience necessary; and to give them the opportunity to meet the best and to learn from the most talented teachers. These, I believe, are justified, and are great ways to express your interest and love for those boys and girls who want to go for their dreams.

ORGANIZING A PRACTICE

Question: I coach several sports, and I'm hoping you can help me to organize and improve the quality of my practices. How can my kids be better prepared and our practice time better used, leading to greater safety?

Answer: Let's face it, in most cases your kids aren't going to have professional coaching in youth sports. The men and women volunteering their time may have experience in the sport they are coaching and may know most of the fundamentals and basic strategies, but they'll probably have little idea of the best ways to organize a practice. This includes not just the warm-ups, drills, and so forth, but, almost more important, how to make the workouts interesting, challenging, instructive, and fun.

While at a national convention for youth coaches in Florida I listened to several speakers whose suggestions I think you'll find invaluable. If you discuss these things with your child's coach prior to the season, they'll give him or her several ideas about running practices, and the guidelines will make their coaching more successful.

The first speaker, Dr. Michael Gray, an exercise physiologist and professor at Northern Kentucky University, spoke concerning intelligent, effective, and safe planning for youth practices. His first point was that all too often adults lose their common sense and tend to ignore the fact that these are youngsters out on the field—*not little adults*. They need special consideration and creative coaching to protect them, teach them effectively, and make their practices fun.

Three primary concerns should be the intensity, frequency, and duration of the workouts. Kids can't be pushed as hard or as long as older athletes, and their attention span is considerably shorter. Therefore, they shouldn't practice more than four or five days a week, and the drills should be short and snappy with lots of rest and teaching periods. This will allow them to catch their breath and focus on the coaching, teaching, and strategy.

Another area stressed by Dr. Gray and with which I

agree strongly is being conscious of the needs and safety factors that are important to each sport. Trying to use some all-encompassing formula for conditioning and coaching for every sport is simply not good enough. Coaches should be sport-specific, looking for the best workouts for their sport; they should be position-specific, teaching and using drills that improve abilities in the different positions called for in that sport; and they should be skill-specific, practicing to build good fundamentals and techniques within each sport.

I learned a few other tips—more philosophic but just as important—from another lecturer, Dr. Robert Elkins, an orthopedic surgeon who has coached kids for fifteen years. He has established three rules that ease the pressures of losing and winning and that assure the coach will be successful in reaching and teaching his or her players.

Rule 1: Make the kids and parents like you. Treat them nicely; be a good guy or gal. Be a leader, but do it with kindness and sincerity.

Rule 2: Make the kids like one another. Make sure the players spend time together away from the field. When it rains, have a get-together at your home, and take them out as a group after some games for ice cream or hamburgers. Also, mix up the players when they're warming up. Don't allow cliques to form. Make sure they get to know all of their teammates.

Rule 3: Get them to like the game. A good coach will make the practices interesting and fun. Spend time explaining strategies and telling big league stories. Don't just work on techniques and give them only tough, structured practices.

If you'll talk to your children's coaches and get them to combine Dr. Gray's practical suggestions with Dr. Elkin's approach, your kids will not only end up better players but their coaches will find the challenge of coaching more fulfilling. Being creative and looking for ways to improve the safety, effectiveness, and fun of practices are very satisfying. The results will be better teams who are closer, more skilled, and happier about the sesaon they spent under a coach's guidance. As a parent you can't ask for any more than that for your kids.

WARM-UPS

It's not necessary for a coach to make a big production out of pre-practice warm-ups and exercises. They needn't last longer than ten or fifteen minutes and shouldn't be hard work or tiring for the players. The team should be stretched, loosened up, and ready for practice, not fatigued or bored. Therefore, the exercise period should be snappy and the number of exercises and repetitions sensible, thereby making the warm-up both enjoyable and functional for your children.

On the Bengals we developed an excellent routine that you may want to suggest to your child's coach. Starting with one lap around the field and then lining up for exercises, each major muscle group and joint should be loosened up and made ready for full-speed competition.

Here are the exercises we do and the order we generally follow:

- Arm circles to loosen up the shoulders.
- Neck circles to stretch and loosen the neck.
- Hamstring: Spread the legs, then reach down and grab the right knee and attempt to put the head on it. No bouncing or bending of the legs should be allowed. Then do the left knee and finish by trying to touch the ground between the legs. Each stretch

should last ten or fifteen seconds. Two to three repetitions are enough.

- Groin: Squat down and put the elbows between the knees and push outward. These should last fifteen or twenty seconds and be repeated two to three times.
- Calf muscles and Achilles tendon: Place one leg back and one forward and lean over the front leg, keeping the back heel on the ground. Then switch the legs and repeat. Fifteen or twenty seconds, and two repetitions each.
- Hip rotation: Place the hands on the hips. Slowly bend forward, legs straight, and rotate all the way around clockwise. Then repeat going counterclockwise. Do five or ten rotations in each direction.
- Go to the ground and do ten sit-ups and ten push-ups and then have your players lie on their backs and roll their legs over their heads, trying to touch their toes on the ground. This will warm up the lower back.
- Players should then stand up and do a little more hamstring work by putting the legs together and trying to touch their toes, their legs remaining straight and no bouncing up and down. The stretch should be smooth, last ten or fifteen seconds, and be repeated three to four times. They might also do another groin exercise such as spreading the legs and then leaning to one side and then the other.
- Finish with ten or fifteen jumping jacks and start practice.

With this routine young athletes will be warmed up and ready to practice but not be tired physically or burned out mentally. One final thing, it's important that the players understand that if they need more stretching to get loose, they should show up a little earlier and do some extra exercises on their own. Every player is different, and some need more stretching than others. This will create good habits when working out on their own and further protect them from injury during games and practices.

SECOND HALF WARM-UPS

Question: Coaches don't seem to warm up the team very much before the second half. They spend all kinds of time before the game, but why so little after halftime?

Answer: Even if the body has been warmed up before the game and during the first half of play, it is essential to relax the muscles after cooling off during halftime. Too many coaches are too casual about this and assume that kids can just take the field again and go at full speed immediately. This isn't true.

While you may not be able to control the coaches, you can teach your children how to get ready for the second half on their own. It's probably better that they learn what their own needs are at an early age anyway because throughout their athletic careers it will be their responsibility to do what is necessary and best for them in preparing for play. Every player is different; some need a lengthy warm-up while others require little.

There are two things your kids should be striving for in preparing for the second half: maintaining a high level of performance and protecting themselves from injury. Stretching is vital to both. After a stressful half of play, the muscles will tighten up during the break. They need to be stretched and lengthened to prevent pulled muscles. Also, more flexibility will lessen the effects of fatigue, which causes many injuries late in ball games.

To perform at their best, athletes need loose muscles and joints that have been prepared for quick starts and stops, hard cuts, and the heavy work load bodies will be called upon to handle. Besides stretching, make sure they work on some agility drills, do some jogging, and then do a few full-speed short sprints and starts out of their stance. Some calisthenics and a few sharp cuts and jumps also will help in final preparation for full-speed execution. Instill in your children the attitude that organized warm-ups with the team are a bonus. They should be ready to go on their own, doing the things that they need most to feel comfortable and confident.

All the above will get your own boys and girls ready for the second half, but I don't think you should stop there. Young athletes need all the information and help they can get. This is why you should talk with your kids' coaches. Make them understand the need for additional warm-ups before the second half so they'll do a better job preparing their teams. As volunteers many of these men and women lack the experience or knowledge that may be critical to their players' performance and health. One thing I have noticed, however, is that they do want to do a good job, and most of them will accept all the assistance and information they can get.

I believe parents' roles in youth sports goes beyond their own children. Anything you can do to help make the experience safer and more fun for everyone involved should be offered. If you can help in any way, do it. Don't underestimate your value or your responsibility to make youth sports better and safer for all kids.

WIND SPRINTS

Question: I hate to run my players to death after practice, but I want to keep them in tip-top condition. Are wind sprints still the answer?

Answer: Wind sprints are one part of maintaining a team's overall conditioning. Too many coaches have misused and overused them, however, to the point where they've actually become punitive instead of functional.

If players are already tired, why should a coach run them to death after practice? Sprints are not mandatory, nor should they ever be used as punishment. Running a team extra hard after a poor performance defeats the whole purpose of running them in the first place. When kids are down, physically or mentally, it should be obvious that pounding them into the ground isn't going to make them a better squad. It's only going to wear them out and make them angry with the coach's poor judgment.

With intelligent, well-organized practices, players will get most of the conditioning they require. They do need to maintain the level of fitness they brought into the season. Making drills snappy, cutting out unnecessary standing around, and having lots of full-speed periods are great ways to keep players in shape and interested during practices.

A good coach can dictate the pace and effectiveness of a workout with careful planning, and an energetic attitude and upbeat practices can quickly eliminate the need for wind sprints. Instead of wasting their energy on minimally productive running, players can be conditioned while honing their skills, learning their plays, and growing athletically. A far superior approach any way you look at it and one that you should make sure your children's coaches are maintaining.

STUCK IN ONE POSITION

Youth coaches should move all of their players to different positions throughout the season, even during each game. It isn't fair or fun to make some kids stay on either defense or offense. They should have a chance to get into the action, whether it's catching, kicking, throwing, blocking, rebounding. Whatever the skills involved in a sport, everybody should have a chance at each of them.

If this isn't the case with your child's coach, then in addition to talking to him or her about a change of philosophy and strategy, you should start working with your child away from the team's practices. Take all the time necessary for full preparation in all of the fundamental skills involved in the sport. If a child is getting cheated out of developing these essentials in organized play, the private work is vital so that the young athlete won't lose ground or confidence for future opportunities.

Understand, however, that it is difficult for a coach to work with fifteen kids and give each enough individual teaching and attention. This gap should be filled by the players' parents. It's up to you to help your child's development. If you don't know enough about a particular sport's techniques, talk to a good coach or get an instructional book to help you, then go out and work with your child. It really is your responsibility.

It is the youth coach's responsibility, however, to make sure the players all have a fair chance to participate and have a good time. By moving the players around, the players' interest will remain longer, they'll learn more about the sport, and their eye-hand coordination and basic athletic skills will be developed more fully. Make sure this happens even if a coach is being irresponsible. Remember,

81

parents and coaches should both be doing everything possible to make youth sports a positive, productive experience. Work together whenever possible.

RUNNING UP SCORES

Running up scores is a surefire way to determine that a coach has a real ego problem and a problem with priorities. Youth sports are supposed to be fun. Running up a score, thus embarrassing the youngsters on the losing squad, is wrong. It is also wrong not to freely substitute and give everyone on the better team a chance to play.

You should sit this type of person down and explain what coaching is all about. This isn't the NCAA, where ratings are involved, or the NFL, where tie breakers concerning point spreads might become significant. Remind the coach about sportsmanship. Youth coaches should not be trying to blow out opponents; they should be doing everything they can to make the game as enjoyable as possible for both teams.

It has become obvious to me that kids don't enjoy these massacres, even as the victors. They become embarrassed for the other team, uncomfortable with their own coach, and lose interest quickly.

A coach who insists on pushing for big margins of victory should be firmly reminded to teach good, sound fundamentals, to explain the various basic rules and strategies of a sport, and to make the players learn about team-oriented goals, working together as individuals for the good of the whole squad and not setting some kind of scoring record.

Pushing for lopsided wins, especially at the expense of substituting for starters and not giving everybody a chance to play, is ridiculous. It shouldn't be tolerated in youth sports.

PUNISHMENT AFTER LOSSES

On the youth levels a coach who begins punishing a team with extra drills, contact, or conditioning because of losses should be removed. This problem is very real when a win-loss record determines a coach's success or failure financially. There is no question that losing is a true test of one's character and very difficult for everyone involved. For a coach above the youth levels, it can be even more taxing because there's a very real and constant pressure to win in order to keep a job, maintain a livelihood and a career with future opportunities. Add ego and pride and the situation can become unbearable and destroy judgment and priorities.

A big part of coaching successfully, however, is the ability to push through the hard times intelligently and divorce oneself from temporary failure. It's quite obvious when a coach is not doing this very well. Working players harder and punishing them with more conditioning after losses only results in exactly what a coach should be working to avoid: tired, injured players and more defeats.

If this situation should ever happen to a child of yours, I suggest that the team captain step forward to talk to the coach and explain the team's feelings as well as, perhaps, those of the parents. If the coach is responsible, then he or she will recognize the error and change tactics immediately. If not, then the team will probably go on losing, the coach will eventually lose the job and, if nothing else, your child should learn a valuable lesson.

There's one thing you should consider carefully: If this coach chooses to ignore players' protests, then you've got to accept it and make the best of it. I know it's difficult to handle someone who's destroying something very important to you or your child, but in this case your only hope is to have the players group together, try to back the coach, and overcome the incompetence.

If everyone quits or protests by not hustling or by having a poor attitude, it's almost certain the team will fail. I'm not just talking about losing every game, I mean failure in the sense that the intangibles, the pulling close during hard times, the loyalty, team concepts, and structure will all crumble, and all will be lost in the process.

It's difficult for youngsters to understand and accept that all persons of authority are not necessarily qualified or successful, but they have to figure it out eventually. Believe me, this problem will be encountered throughout life no matter what business they're involved in, so if your children can learn to handle this difficult and painful situation correctly, they'll have a head start on others.

5

Nutrition

Questions: What do pro players eat before games? Are there things that will make me play better and last longer in soccer? I get tired in the second half.

Answers: There's no magic pre-game meal that will make your children all-stars. In fact, chances are greater they'll eat something that will hurt their play rather than help it.

The first thing you must realize is that it takes the body from one and a half to two days to change a meal into usable energy. Therefore, pre-game food won't have much impact on endurance or energy level that day. Even so, choosing what your children eat is important because the wrong food can upset their stomachs, drawing too much blood from the muscles to the stomach and, ultimately, hurting the quality of their play.

In general, try to serve the meal at least two hours before a contest. On the Bengals, as on all professional football teams, we always allow four hours for digestion. Go for light meals rich in carbohydrates, such as soups and sandwiches for afternoon or night games and maybe pancakes or fruits in the morning. Some other examples of good pre-game foods are juices, low-fat yogurt, whole wheat bread, cereal and skim milk, and low-fat protein items such as chicken, turkey, eggs, and low-fat cottage cheese.

Make sure to serve foods they're used to; don't try new items they're unaccustomed to handling. Trying some new, exotic dish on the day of a game is too big a gamble. Confidence and comfort are important factors, so foods they enjoy and eat often are preferable.

Avoid hard-to-digest foods such as steaks and high-sugar items. They should drink lots of water, tea (decaffeinated), or fruit juices. Myths about the benefits of quick energy items such as honey, candy bars, and soft drinks are untrue. In fact, these items can hurt a performance. Concentrated amounts of sugar must be broken down by the body, which draws fluids to the stomach and can lead to dehydration. Also, the quick energy high can lead to an abrupt crash and actually take away from endurance and, in fact, the ability to perform at the highest level possible.

It's necessary to stress that every athlete is different. The guidelines I am giving you are generally accepted by trainers, coaches, and nutritionists on the highest levels of competition. However, there are athletes who eat all the wrong things—greasy chicken, hamburgers, french fries, milkshakes—and still excel out on the field.

What you must do is find out what works best for your kids on game days. What gives them the most confidence and the fewest physical problems? These are questions only you can answer, and these answers can be discovered only through experience and experimentation.

Another thing to consider: Since it takes so long for food to be converted to usable energy by the body, it should be obvious how important diet is throughout the week. Eating good, nutritious meals every day will elminate most of the worries on game day. Too many athletes fret about what they should eat before a game and neglect proper eating when it counts most, which is all the time.

Basically, a pre-game meal should be no more important than any other meal unless the activity involved calls for unusual endurance, such as bicycling, long-distance swimming, or a marathon. For sports such as soccer, football, basketball, and baseball, endurance will come from training and overall conditioning, not from what an athlete eats before a game.

PRE-GAME SWEETS

Questions: Will eating candy bars or other sweets just before competition give me more energy to play? And if I eat them during halftime, will they help me play better at the end of the game when I'm usually tired?

Answers: Candy bars do not provide "instant energy." I'm a little embarrassed because in the past I've eaten them during the halftimes of NFL games and in volleyball tournaments, thinking they'd give me more energy and stamina. Let's shatter this myth once and for all.

Eating anything with a high sugar content an hour or less before strenuous exercise can actually hinder performance rather than help it. Without getting too technical, these snacks are absorbed quickly into the bloodstream, triggering the body to release large amounts of insulin. Combined with exercise, this can lead to hypoglycemia (low blood sugar). Some of the symptoms are loss of coordination, shaking, hunger, and light-headedness.

If your children eat a candy bar while exercising—such as between plays, during timeouts, or at halftime—it's going to sit in their stomachs and draw fluids from their bodies to dilute the mass of sugar. This can bloat the stomach and lead to dehydration. Since it takes some time for the sugar to be absorbed, there's very little immediate gain.

As you can see, sugar snacks just prior to competition are not going to help endurance, enegy level, or performance, so your kids should avoid eating them.

VITAMINS

Question: Will massive doses of vitamins help my children's performance or their athletic development?

Answer: Vitamins are now so popular and commercialized that most of us have lost track of what they are and what they really do. We all require vitamins in small amounts for normal growth and good health. They are found in enzymes that regulate chemical reactions in our bodies, and since we cannot manufacture them, we must obtain them through our diet or supplemental sources.

We are constantly being bombarded by advertisements and personal testimonials of the great effects vitamins have on health and physical performance. The truth is, most of us meet our vitamin requirements through a normal, balanced diet, and there is no basis for believing that an athlete's needs are any greater than a nonathlete's.

Medical sources have repeatedly stated that massive vitamin supplements will not improve strength, performance, or endurance, and they will not prevent injuries or even common colds. Why then are so many athletes taking so many vitamins? Because athletes are always looking for a competitive edge, something that will help make them a little bit better or stronger than their teammates and competitors.

One of the great consistencies of the athletic drive and mind is that if two of something is good, then twenty is ten times better, and so on, whether it has been medically proven or not. This thinking leads to tremendous doses and abuses of substances that have never been shown to increase health or performance.

Major influences have been the theories of Dr. Linus Pauling, two-time Nobel Prize winner and advocate of huge quantities of vitamin C for prevention of colds, cancer, and emotional disease. I admit I took tons of vitamin C for a while, thinking I had found the magical cure for health. Nice try, but Dr. Pauling's "findings" have never been proven through controlled, scientific research. It has been found, however, that side effects such as diarrhea and kidney stones may result from large doses of this vitamin.

These megadoses of vitamin C are now being taken with other vitamins that are supposed to increase strength, stamina, and energy levels. The following two questions address this absurdity.

Question: Will vitamin B-12 shots really give you more energy? I hear that many professional athletes use them.

Answer: If many professional athletes use vitamin B-12 shots, all they're doing is putting unnecessary holes in their behinds. Except for long-time pure vegetarians and individuals suffering from a rare form of anemia, these shots have no proven medical value.

Movies like *North Dallas Forty*, in which some of the players received B-12 shots, and the fact that an athlete such as Muhammad Ali had a shot two days before his fights have given B-12 injections an undeserved reputation as energy boosters.

If your children suffer from chronic fatigue, they're probably suffering from a shortage of potassium in the body. They should start eating large quantities of fresh fruit and vegetables. If after a short while fatigue continues, then they should be taken to a doctor.

If your kids are healthy and just looking for a boost of some sort, forget about B-12 shots. The only benefit they'll receive will be psychological; they won't be helped physically.

Question: Will vitamin E in large doses help my stamina and strength? I've heard that it does, and I want to know if it's worth taking.

Answer: Though it has been pushed and publicized as the great sexual and energy drug of the '70s and '80s, it has never been proven that vitamin E aids either potency or athletic performance. In fact, those athletes who are injecting the stuff in great doses may be endangering their health, and the vitamin may be toxic in great quantities.

The truth about vitamin E is that researchers have not been able to determine what role it plays in our bodies. I would recommend receiving the vitamin through a normal diet. Margarine, soybeans, wheat germ, and cereal will more than meet normal needs.

Strength and stamina will be improved only by working out consistently and diligently and by a well-balanced diet. Vitamin E supplements for a healthy athlete are unnecessary, a waste of money, and potentially dangerous. Steer clear of them.

SAFELY GAINING WEIGHT

Question: I'm eleven years old and very skinny. I eat all the time, but I just can't put on any weight. I've seen ads for protein drinks and pills for gaining weight. Will any of these do me any good?

Answer: Gaining weight is a major concern for many young athletes. I can tell you that as a six-foot, 135-pound varsity quarterback in high school, it sure was one of my biggest priorities. About all I thought of was how skinny I was, how bad I looked in clothes, and how I was willing to do just about anything to bulk up some. Well, I was fortunate that my desire was kept in line by an intelligent family doctor and my parents. I was told steroids were the only answer and seriously considered taking them until advised against them by my physician, who even back then was aware of their dangerous side effects.

My parents did go out and buy some of the highly publicized wonder protein drinks and pills, but they had little impact, though I dedicated myself to forcing the ill-tasting stuff down my throat day after day.

As simple and as unsatisfying as it may sound, I found out through the years that the best and safest way to gain weight is through a good, well-balanced diet. Young athletes should stay away from the shortcuts they might read or hear about.

Don't let them fool themselves and count on low-nutrition, greasy fast foods and snacks such as soft drinks, candy bars, or potato chips. These do little other than fill them up; they contain what actually amounts to empty calories because the body cannot use the ingredients for anything but accumulation of fat. Rather, make sure their diet includes items from all the major food groups: fish, fowl, meat, cereal, milk and milk products, and plenty of fresh fruits and vegetables. They should eat three square meals a day, every day, with only healthy snacks in between.

The best thing your kids can do is keep working on their conditioning and athletic skills, and on their ability to handle competitive sports. As they grow older and their bodies mature, they'll put on weight through exercise and good consistent eating.

Remember one very important fact: It's not how much athletes weigh that matters but what percentage they're carrying of muscle as opposed to body fat. Even in football, players are better off at a lighter, more muscular weight than carrying a few extra pounds, which are basically just fat. Don't allow your kids to get hung up on how much they weigh but rather have them concentrate on conditioning, flexibility, strength, and developing athletic skills. These will prove to be far more important and influential in determining how well they perform.

WEIGHT-GAIN WASTE

Question: I worked hard over the past year to put on weight, but I've found that I've lost some speed and quickness, and even my conditioning has suffered. I'm not fat, I added muscles, and I'm definitely stronger, but instead of making me a better player, the extra weight has hurt me. Is this common?

Answer: Adding weight is probably the most overblown concern in sports. Putting on weight for weight's sake, to be statistically superior or to look more impressive on paper, is a waste of time and effort.

Every athlete should try to find an optimum weight he or she can carry that allows peak performance with maximum protection. This is strictly an individual thing. No coach or player can arbitrarily decide that, say, thirty additional pounds will make a player a better performer. It's quite often true that too much weight, even if it is muscle, can slow down an athlete, hurt endurance, and hinder play rather than enhance it.

What matters most is not how much your child weighs but how well he or she performs. Sacrificing athleticism and conditioning for size is a poor exchange. Also, added strength and muscle without a corresponding gain in flexibility actually works against an athlete.

Being an awesome physical specimen may be flattering to one's ego, but it'll never replace skills, desire, and mental preparation. Many professional teams have been burned by high draft choices who had perfect physiques, could jump high, run fast, lift tons of iron but, unfortunately, couldn't play the sport they were being paid to excel in.

Make sure your kids understand that they shouldn't concern themselves so much with physical statistics. Instead they should concentrate on becoming the best athletes possible, applying their concentration to those sports most important to them and grading themselves on results, not on a little needle on a weight scale.

SAFELY LOSING WEIGHT

Questions: Are there safe ways for young athletes to lose weight? My son wrestles and is always starving himself and taking steam baths to make his weight. Is this dangerous?

Answers: Anyone who uses starvation or dehydration to reach a certain weight is gambling with both health and performance. There are no secret, easy diets that will help cut corners and reach a desired weight.

Make sure your children avoid "fad" diets. These generally eliminate carbohydrate-rich foods that athletes need for strength and endurance. They also radically change the caloric intake and can result in personality changes and physical weakness. They don't result in fat loss but muscle deterioration and water loss, both of which are critical to any athlete and particularly those competing in strength and stamina sports.

Let me use the high school senior wrestling season of former Bengals All-Pro middle linebacker Jim Leclair to illustrate this. He finished football at 205 pounds, quickly lost 15 pounds, and competed at the 190-pound classification. In preparation for the state competition he dropped another 23 pounds to make the 167-pound competition.

He'd had a fine season at 190, but the additional weight he dropped ruined his season. He became drained physically and emotionally. His entire life was affected. Obviously his eating habits were radically altered. He was hungry all the time; he would skip meals, then devour a huge feast after a match, only to starve himself again prior to the next meet. This terrible cycle continued week after week.

By the time the state finals rolled around, his energy level was low and his strength diminished; he'd lost his endurance, and his enthusiasm and enjoyment of the sport had disappeared. He looks back on this period of his life and can't believe he put himself through the pain, personality change, and fatigue he experienced, especially since his performance suffered in the long run.

Your kids should concern themselves with reducing their percentage of body fat, not just weight loss. After setting a realistic goal, they should plan to lose two or three pounds a week, using patience because losing more than this is not healthy. Remind them that just as it took time to put on the weight, it will take time to take it off.

Don't allow them to change their eating habits drastically. Instead they should cut down on the amounts of their favorite foods—maybe two hamburgers instead of three, or three pancakes instead of five, for example. Encourage them to eat more fruits, vegetables, and low-calorie foods instead of greasy, creamy, or fatty items.

As they diet make sure they don't skip meals. Many times people become ravenous at night after missing earlier meals, and then they splurge—which is much worse than just eating at consistent times.

Another area in which they can benefit from better planning is their fluid intake. Stress that water is the best liquid they can drink to quench their thirst and replace the body fluids lost through perspiration. Soft drinks are full of calories, and selecting water instead will help their diet as well as be better for them overall.

Finally, exercise can help the dieting process tremendously. Have your kids run a few extra laps or walk to places they might ordinarily be driven to. This will not only help their conditioning but help shed a few more of those tough pounds.

Don't allow them to ever get involved in any starvation and steam bath routines. Besides being dangerous, these will leave young athletes weakened, thus hurting their performances and increasing the chances of injury. Patience, an intelligent diet, and a well-planned training program are the only safe, effective answers to losing weight.

6

Health and Safety

There are many danger areas in sports where knowledge-able parents can protect their children from ignorant, irre-sponsible coaches or from overzealous, determined athletes themselves. Understanding the necessity of fluids during competition, the need for intelligent, conservative approaches to weight-gain and weight-loss, the dangers of throwing a baseball or certain football drills are all the responsibilities of good parents.

It's not enough to simply tell your kids "steroids are bad." You have to prove it to them, give them reasons for what you're telling them. Today's athletes are hungry for success. They're maturing at younger ages. The competi-tion is the toughest ever, and for those looking for an extra edge, the temptations and pitfalls grow ever more promi-nent. You have to provide perspective and outline when overwork has reached the law of diminished return; you have to help guide your kids to their goals.

There are still too many abuses in our youth sports. Kids still die because of bad coaches, sometimes because of masochistic workouts in heat or by using unsafe practice drills that have no place in athletics. Athletes, too, are to blame. They experiment with substances such as steroids or amphetamines, which they hope will make them perform better. These, our best and brightest kids, are willing to do anything to succeed.

Don't lose touch. Don't simply pass on your responsibility to men and women who want winners or who need victories to satisfy their own egos, to keep their jobs, or to move on to better positions. Watch practices and read basic health and diet books. Never stop governing or understanding what your boys and girls are doing in their efforts to improve. YOURS IS AN ONGOING JOB, ONE THAT BECOMES INCREASINGLY VITAL AS YOUR CHILDREN MOVE UP THE ATHLETIC LADDER.

DRINKING WATER

Questions: I am sixteen and play football, basketball, and track. I can't understand why we can't drink water during practice but at games we can have all we want. Is this safe, and can you tell me why it is or isn't?

Answers: I can remember kneeling down to await my one squirt of water in the tiny paper cup the coaches provided us in my collegiate days at Harvard. I'd look around at my teammates, lined up on either side of me, future lawyers, doctors, professors, and politicians, each appearing like a beggar or wino hoping for an extra drop or two. The absurdity of this scene during the terrible heat and humidity of preseason two-a-day practices at one of the leading educational institutions in the world still frightens me. We needed water, lots of it, but were denied for ignorant, dangerous traditions.

Even worse, this continued in the NFL. We weren't allowed *any* water until 1980 at Bengals practices. Can you imagine professional football players tipping youngsters to sneak them some ice cubes to quench their thirst? Well, we did this until they finally supplied water containers.

It's high time that this irrational stance taken by many coaches regarding no fluids during practice is buried once and for all. This form of discipline, supposedly designed to make players tougher, is extremely dangerous and harmful to an athlete's health.

Water is the fuel that makes our bodies run. When we exercise we lose a great deal of fluid. It is very important that it be replaced quickly for health and safety reasons. If not, an athlete will lose strength, timing, and judgment, and his or her performance can suffer.

The danger of intensive practice in high temperatures combined with physical fatigue and dehydration can seriously limit the body's ability to respond to stress. These factors can lead to heat exhaustion, or heat stroke, and death. These occur when an athlete has overtaxed the ability of the heart and lungs to handle heat and humidity while playing.

Warning signs are a weak but fast heartbeat, skin that becomes cold and clammy to the touch and, because of poor circulation, dizziness and/or fainting. The necessity of rest and adequate fluids must be responded to immediately by coaches.

As for prevention, a thorough preseason physical fitness program would help the athlete adjust to the sun, heat, and humidity. Coaches absolutely should have mandatory water breaks during practice, with fluids available when the players need them. This need not be disruptive. There are always moments when individuals can get a quick drink and not affect the flow of practice.

It has been proven that, both prior to and during play, taking more water than is expected to be lost will lead to maximum performance. For example, it is estimated that there is a loss of one to two liters of water per hour during early-season football practices.

It's obvious that, particularly in hot weather, fluids should be readily available to the athletes during games and practices. They should be made aware of fluids and encouraged to drink them whenever needed. They shouldn't feel like weaklings or babies because they're thirsty. In fact, coaches should be pleased that they *are* thirsty because it indicates the athletes are working hard.

If coaches ever deny your children water during practice, you should speak to them in a hurry and insist that they stop this barbaric approach to coaching. This could mean saving a youngster's life—kids are still tragically dying every season from heatstroke. Don't allow this to happen.

AVOIDING HEAT EXHAUSTION

Questions: I read where another boy died in preseason football practice. What can I do to prevent this from happening to my son?

My son gets unusually tired after practicing in hot weather and loses his appetite. He then loses weight and strength. Is there anything he can do?

Answers: I've received many letters from concerned parents whose children have been involved in heavy exercise in extreme heat, particularly preseason football practice. Many others have asked about the dangers and ways to prevent dehydration, heat exhaustion, and worse. They've asked about salt pills, proper diet, fluids, and overcoming the fatigue their young athletes suffer after lengthy battles with the sun and humidity.

There are four main elements that must be replaced after exercising in hot weather because they are lost in great quantities through the related heavy perspiration: water (fluids), sodium (salt), potassium, and magnesium.

Replacing fluids is absolutely essential. Have your son or daughter drink heavily before the workout. This over-hydration, along with water breaks during practice, can help prevent dehydration. Also, lots of fluids should be taken between and after heavy workouts. If your child's coach doesn't allow water breaks, do whatever it takes to make him. Nondrinking in heat is not a form of discipline; it's plain stupid, masochistic, and extremely dangerous to an athlete's health and life.

Replacing sodium or salt is a little trickier. Too little salt in the body can result in high blood pressure, clots in the bloodstream, and heat exhaustion. Too much salt can cause an athlete to urinate more often, depriving the body of more fluids, and can lead to heat exhaustion, heat stroke, clotting, and even heart attacks. Most physicians and trainers recommend adding some extra salt to food during heavy periods of exercise. Your children's taste buds will let them know if more salt is needed by their bodies, although in most cases they will receive more than enough in their normal diets. Salt pills bypass this natural gauge and are not recommended by most authorities.

When we're thirsty we drink, when we need more sodium we crave salty foods, but there are no natural bodily signs to tell an individual to increase his or her intake of potassium. When the body is low in potassium, however, an athlete will feel tired, weak, and irritable. Good sources to replace this lost mineral are all fruits, particularly bananas, and juices, vegetables, molasses, and wheat germ.

Low magnesium levels can lead to chronic fatigue and muscle cramps. This mineral is found in dairy products, oatmeal, meats, peanuts, peas, and rice.

It's obvious that a good, well-balanced diet will provide an athlete with the necessary minerals to replace those lost through heavy perspiration. The problem is that many athletes do not feel like eating the right foods when they need them most. Hard workouts in the sun really do drain a player. The combination of fatigue and drinking large amounts of fluids generally leads to a loss of appetite.

Make sure your children eat consistently and as fully as possible after hard practices. It is vital that they drink plenty of fluids, but don't allow their thirst to destroy their appetites. Be conscientious about providing meals that include items from all of the basic food groups, and keep after your children to eat and drink even when they don't feel like it.

HOT WEATHER PRECAUTIONS

Question: I'd like to know the best ways to handle the extreme heat of early season games and practices. Are there little things you do on the pro level that help?

Answer: Besides good conditioning as a basis, intelligence and common sense can combine to go a long way in preventing cramps, fatigue, and heat exhaustion.

First of all, a coach should approach practice differently

when it's hot, particularly late in the week. Players should be worked hard on the early days, but that work load should be cut down as the game approaches. Keeping them off the field the day before a contest and substituting meetings in place of the usual workout can make a big difference in the later stages of the game.

The importance of taking extra fluids throughout the week should be emphasized. Players should be drinking heavily for several days prior to a game, not simply before and during it. If they try to drink too much before a contest, they'll generally become sluggish and feel uncomfortable, and their performance will suffer accordingly.

Talk to the coach if necessary and suggest that he or she change pre-game warm-ups in extreme heat. Going on the field later than normal and staying out there a few minutes less are important. It doesn't take as much time or effort to loosen up and keep the muscles warmed up when it's hot. The athletes don't have to dress in full uniform until gametime. Players shouldn't be worn out before the contest. If possible, they should wear mesh jerseys and cutoff shirts under their outerwear instead of long-sleeved, heavy clothing. This will help cool the midriff area.

During halftime they should change into clean, dry undergarments and pull their long socks down to their ankles. Sitting and resting while drinking as many fluids as possible are all helpful in playing the second half.

Have towels soaked in ice water for players to put on their heads and on exposed skin. Have ice water for them to drink; it's absorbed into the bloodstream and cools the body much faster and more effectively than warm fluids. Don't allow them to take salt pills; these can actually cause dehydration.

Finally, substituting players intelligently is critical. For instance, if a receiver runs a deep pattern, someone else should go in for the next play to give him a little rest. Playing as many players as possible, spreading the work load, and preserving the starters for the fourth quarter when they'll need their concentration and strength most are all signs that your children have a well-versed, intelligent coach guiding them.

STEROIDS

Questions: I've read about the dangers of anabolic steroids, but now I hear there are new, manufactured kinds that are safe. Are they?

Will steroids help me get bigger muscles and greatly increase my weight? By not using them am I giving my competitors an advantage over me?

If steroids are so bad, how come so many athletes are using them?

Answers: Over the past few years there has been a tremendous backlash against steroid use of any kind, in any fashion, to any degree. Athletes have been stripped of their medals at the Pan Am games and at the Olympics, and even more forceful action is being discussed such as lifetime expulsion from competition. In addition, the National Collegiate Athletic Association (NCAA) banned a number of football players from postseason Bowl games, including Oklahoma's All-American, Brian Bosworth, for testing positive for steroids.

Doctors, athletes, and trainers have stepped forward with warnings of the very real dangers of steroid usage, and countless articles, books, and television reports have chronicled the health hazards and atrocities involved with their abuse. And yet I'm still receiving tons of letters from frightened parents, young athletes who want to gain weight and strength, and others looking to keep up with their competition. All of them argue or ask if there really is a danger or if it has been blown out of proportion, and they want to know what effect steroids will have on their health and performance.

Let me quote Dan B. Riley, the conditioning coach of the Washington Redskins: "I believe that *any* use of an anabolic steroid by a healthy athlete is *abuse*. Let me say it loud and clear: Steroids are *dangerous*; they are potential killers. That's why it's illegal to purchase them without a doctor's prescription, and that's why any physician who prescribes steroids to a healthy individual should be prosecuted for criminal malpractice." He adds that a coach is "professionally, morally, and legally responsible for the well-being of his athletes. And that means he cannot encourage or condone the use of steroids." He also emphasizes that in his experience most athletes who use them, despite all the warnings and the danger, do so because they're looking for an edge or because they're uninformed or misinformed.

Let me state it clearly for everyone. Weight lifters' claims of increased muscle weight and strength through the use of steroids have never been substantiated. On the contrary, two major studies conducted at UCLA and Long Beach State College have shown that any weight gain is attributed to increased retention of water, not extra muscle. And no strength increases have ever been proven.

Beyond this, and more important, serious medical side effects have been found. These include liver and kidney damage, excessive red blood cells, prostate damage, impotence, cancerous tumors, raised blood pressure, and complications to the heart and arteries.

It should be obvious that any use or experimentation of any kind with any steroid of any type is insane. I agree with

Dan Riley that doctors and coaches should be held legally responsible for the continued use of these potential killers. For the athletes there can be no more excuses. Steroids are illegal without a prescription and dangerous to the point of death. Tell your children to forget them. In fact, work tirelessly to make sure they're never seduced into even thinking about using them.

RUNNING PROBLEMS

Question: Do you think it's safe for teenagers to run so much on asphalt? My son is on the cross-country team and often complains of pain in his legs after doing "roadwork," and my daughter, who jogs to keep fit, has had problems too.

Answer: There are many factors that distance runners, particularly young and inexperienced ones, overlook in their workouts that can lead to discomfort and injury. The human body was built to run on softer surfaces. It takes time and conditioning to handle the pounding and difficulty of running on asphalt, especially when hill climbing and decending are involved.

Give this checklist to your children to review if they begin to suffer pain after their workouts.

1. Have I increased my distances too rapidly? Most people begin by running around the track a few times. Running in circles becomes boring, so they head out on the streets. Many tend to run too far, too fast, without allowing their bodies to build up a tolerance to the new, greater pounding.

2. Have I added another athletic activity? Sometimes a runner does fine until another activity is added such as basketball or aerobics. Soreness and injury may result from the added stress and burden.

3. Have I changed my style of running? Many runners who start running with a new partner fall into a faster pace on more challenging ground. Running up and down hills, for instance, puts more stress on one's body than a level track. Also, some roads have higher crowns, and this can cause the runner to put more strain on the leg nearer the curb, as it will be absorbing a greater percentage of the shock.

4. Am I stretching enough before and after running? Warming up and cooling down properly are important in distance running. Make sure to stretch before and after, and walk some after finishing.

5. Am I running equally on both sides of the road? Because most roads are crowned for drainage, the outside leg will be stressed because it hits lower and must absorb more impact. This adds up as the mileage increases and the workouts continue.

6. Running on asphalt is undeniably tougher on the body than running on a nice, level athletic track. If a runner's legs continue to be sore, he or she might be heading for injury, and I would suggest either cutting down drastically on the mileage, finding dirt trails to run on, or returning to the track.

Shoes are critical in distance running. I cannot recommend one brand or style because everyone's feet are different. I would suggest going to a reputable sporting goods store and having your kids try on several well-known name brands. They'll all feel different, so have them continue to explore until they find the most comfortable pair for them.

The shoes should fit snugly but still allow normal toe movement and circulation.

Shoes control the angle at which the foot hits the ground. This will be affected by the thickness, width, and height of the sole, the size of the arch, the inner padding, and even the type of lacing. All of these factors are important in preventing hip, back, and knee problems, many of which relate to the foot hitting the ground improperly.

Shoes are like artificial feet; they should absorb the force and cushion the rest of the body from the terrible pounding it receives in running distances. Make sure your boys and girls choose their running shoes carefully, and if at all possible spend the extra money to get the highest quality.

Finally, besides the physical demands of cross-country and long-distance jogging, there can be tremendous mental strain. Don't allow your kids to run so much that they burn out on the activity and give it up prematurely. Help them to steer clear of getting frustrated or hurt because of overzealousness before they're ready. Patience and consistency are truly the keys in distance running.

WEIGHT LOSS IN WRESTLING

Weight loss in wrestling, particularly on the high school level, has always been surrounded by controversy. Athletes and coaches have used and encouraged methods such as fasting and dehydration to reach weight classifications one to three (seven to twenty-one pounds) below the normal weight. The belief has always been that the wrestlers will then have an advantage over their "smaller" opponents.

This thinking has been proven ridiculous. For one thing, since many other competitors are trying to accomplish the same thing, what can be gained? It'll just be a wash since everyone will be attempting the same strategy, right? And, more important, this unnecessary weight loss in already well-conditioned athletes is dangerous, potentially harmful to growth and, ultimately, a liability to performance and health.

Fasting or aggressive dieting, especially in active youngsters, can result in neglect of basic nutritional needs at the most critical growth and maturation periods of their lives.

Wearing plastic clothes while working out or taking lengthy saunas and steam baths in order to drop some extra water weight has many dangers. The kidneys can be impaired by the reduced plasma flow infiltration. Additionally, more muscle weight than fat will be lost using these techniques, thus hurting the competitor's conditioning.

Loss of strength after lengthy dieting and sweating sessions has been documented. Also, case studies have shown emotional stability being affected by these activities. Athletes can become irritable, suffer "flat" performances, have drastic mood swings, and feel fatigued much of the time.

All of the above adds up to an obvious conclusion: Coaches and athletes should realize that losing weight unnecessarily in order to compete in lower weight classifications is a poor idea. Logically, does it make sense to risk your health and possibly retard your physical growth, especially when the edge you're seeking is offset by the fact that you'll be battling your opponent with less strength, endurance, and skill than you possess at your natural weight?

Since athletes are always searching for ways to improve performance, to gain an edge over their competition, they make many important decisions that can affect their health. It's this drive to excel that results in the use of steroids, drugs, and other abusive substances that shouldn't be a part of sports. Wrestlers dropping pounds to reach lower levels, where they believe they'll have a better chance to win, can be just as irresponsible and dangerous as these more publicized, feared threats to mental and physical health.

It's time for coaches, parents, and teammates to stop the ignorant, misconceived notion of unnecessary weight loss in wrestling. It's not only hurting the competitors, it's ruining the public conception of the sport and threatening its integrity.

ORTHOTICS

Question: I've had trouble with leg pain, and my feet hurt after I play hard or run too much. My friends have mentioned things called orthotics. What are they?

Answer: Orthotics are shoe inserts that many athletes are now using to help treat and prevent injuries to their hips, legs, knees, feet, and back.

I personally wear them everywhere, even in my dress shoes, because I've had a great deal of trouble with my feet. Before orthotics I had difficulty getting up in the morning and walking because my feet hurt so much. Now I can go out and play basketball, volleyball, tennis, and even jog long distances with very little discomfort during or after the activities.

Orthotics, obtained from podiatrists or orthopedists, are made from casts of the patient's foot. They are quite expensive—some are around $100.

Arch supports and inserts are available from pharmacists, however, and these might be adequate for your child. Try these first—they're considerably cheaper—but if the problem persists, see a foot specialist.

ASTHMA

Many parents, coaches, and children ask me whether or not youngsters with asthma should get involved in athletics. The parents are worried about the effects on their sons' and daughters' health; the coaches are concerned with the special treatment their players may need; and the kids want to know what they can do to play the sports they love.

Thinking about it, the number of questions is not surprising since approximately 2 percent of our population suffers from asthma or related conditions involving bronchospasms.

Most physicians I've talked to have said that in approaching sports with children who suffer from asthma, the main thrust should be participation over excellence, although some top athletes including Olympians have been asthmatics. The primary goals should be education, fitness, and social involvement; too many asthmatics have been unnecessarily deprived of these elements.

Continued supervision is called for because asthma cannot be eliminated; it is a lifelong problem. Positive help and reinforcement from parents, coaches, and doctors are important in helping to overcome the physical limitations and mental stress of being left out or being handled differently. Learning to cope with asthma's limitations is also important; otherwise the child will feel inadequate and left out not only on the playing field but also socially.

Exercise can definitely affect asthma. E.I.A. (Exercise Induced Asthma) is a real and widespread problem that can be overcome. After being educated about their condition, children should begin their activities slowly, building a good foundation of fitness under the doctor's guidance. They must accept the fact that such things as cold weather, altitude, pollen, pollution, and infections can all influence their participation and necessary medication on any given day. Even highly conditioned asthmatics and their coaches must be aware that performance and endurance can be greatly affected when any of these adverse elements is present. IT IS ESSENTIAL FOR ATHLETES TO USE THEIR MEDI-CATION CONSISTENTLY AND PROPERLY. Overuse in difficult conditions can trigger an attack, and not taking their medication in the belief that they're in good enough shape without it can be equally dangerous.

There are many problems beyond physical considerations when working with asthmatic children. Overprotective parents can negatively affect a child's physical development by discouraging their participation. On the other side of the coin, children can use their condition to get out of gym class or physical exertion that would benefit them greatly. Coaches and doctors should tell a patient about all of the positive gains to be achieved by playing sports, but they should also prepare the child for the risks. Psychologically it's difficult to handle being pulled out of a game with fatigue or a coughing attack or being allowed only limited participation. But physically real are the chances of a severe attack that can result in hospitalization, although occurrences are rare and usually only when an underlying infection compounds the problem.

Yet the benefits of playing sports can far outweigh the limitations and risks for those suffering from asthma. Besides feeling better physically and mentally because of improved fitness, children can enhance their self-image and social acceptance by participating in athletics. An exercise program based on what is acceptable for each child's condition can be therapeutic and lead to experiencing life more fully, with all of its competitiveness, excitement, failure, and success.

DANGEROUS FOOTBALL DRILLS

I constantly receive letters from concerned parents and players who are worried about some of the drills being used at football practices. In most cases these blocking and tackling exercises have been proven ineffective in teaching sound fundamentals and are, without question, unsafe, particularly on the youth level.

One of the most popular is nicknamed "the bull in the ring." In this drill a player is encircled by the team and the coach yells out one or more numbers. The players wearing those numbers then run at the man in the center and try to hit him. It's his job to protect himself and ward off their blows, delivering one of his own if possible. This exercise is ridiculous and barbaric. It teaches nothing and is dangerous because the player in the center is often hit in the back and is blindsided. Injuries have been frequent and serious. I know of one case in which a boy was killed by a hit to his back while involved in this drill.

Any coach who uses "the bull in the ring" is irresponsible and should be seriously reprimanded and the exercise stopped immediately. This type of brutality and unnecessary danger should not be a part of football.

Another drill that should be curtailed, especially in youth football, is one in which two players lie on their backs with their helmets almost touching. One is the blocker, the other a tackler. Behind the blocker there is generally a runner who must maneuver between two blocking dummies and avoid being tackled. At the sound of the whistle, the two principals jump up and try to either prevent or make the tackle. The problem is that in such a cramped space there are too many injuries, either through contact or by falling awkwardly over bodies or on the dummies. Countless knee, ankle, and shoulder injuries have resulted.

A major problem with this exercise is that coaches often create mismatches between the two players lying on their backs. One may be considerably stronger, the other much quicker. This can lead to an injury. Often, too, the runners get injured because they're not really running hard but trying to avoid getting hurt.

Practicing cross body blocks "live" is another unnecessary risk. It's just as effective to teach this skill using a standing dummy. This gives the players a feel for the proper techniques and timing. Using "live" blocking between two players can result in injuries to the player being blocked, who is not really playing football but trying to protect himself, as well as to the blocker, who hasn't learned how to hit and roll out of the block safely. This block is dangerous at all times, especially to the knees, and should be used minimally and properly.

Gang tackling a player with the ball in practice to toughen him up or as punishment for fumbling should never be permitted. Again, part of the risk is that the tacklers are trying to protect themselves, and they don't really want to beat up on a teammate. If a coach ever endorses this type of exercise, he belongs in another profession. Players and parents should unite in directing him out of football.

There are other potentially harmful drills which I have either experienced or been informed of by readers. Anytime a coach endangers the health of a player unnecessarily, he is wrong. Teaching blocking and tackling properly can be done in most cases with either dummies, pads, or using "form" practice. This is half-speed technique work in which the players hit, lift, and finish their blocking and tackling without the other player even hitting the ground. Full-speed hitting is never used.

This type of coaching will lead to better, more consistent play and more important, can cut down on injury. With less needless, risky contact, players will be fresher at gametime. To deliberately place players in jeopardy through drills or exercises such as those outlined is unforgivable. This type of coaching should be stamped out for good, with no exceptions.

SCRIMMAGING IN FOOTBALL

If you look at the different levels of competition in tackle football, in most cases the amount of full contact during the week progressively lessens as a player moves from youth through high school, college, and the pros. I believe the lower levels are wrong in scrimmaging and conducting drills that involve "live" hitting during the week once the season has begun.

While it is vital that kids learn the proper fundamentals of blocking and tackling, this should be stressed during the preseason. After the games begin, however, the players should be protected from unnecessary injuries while their bodies recover from each contest. Besides the obvious threat involved in any full contact situation, there is a cumulative effect that can lead to injuries through fatigue and overwork.

Football players should concentrate more on fundamentals and strategy when preparing for each game. Coaches who insist on running scrimmages every day in addition to installing plays and practicing the basic skills of the sport are wrong. There are ways of teaching blocking and tackling that don't involve all-out contact. Working on the proper techniques using dummies and half-speed form drills, stopping once initial contact is made, have almost eliminated the need for scrimmaging.

Although players in the NFL do have great experience and talent, the true reason their coaches use a minimum of contact is that it's too dangerous. Coaches on the lower levels should consider this and act accordingly.

One day before our opening game, when I was a junior in high school, our coach made the team suddenly hit whoever was around them when he blew his whistle. As a result our star running back was hurt and couldn't play for a few weeks. This eventually cost us a shot at the league title. How foolish that was, and yet things like this still go on.

Scrimmaging day in and day out is a poor philosophy. I've never understood why coaches would risk their team's health and their own jobs through the midweek full-scrimmage routine. What can they possibly hope to gain? Their players are tired, beat up, and mentally down even if they are lucky enough to come through the week unscathed. Worse, any players injured during the scrimmages are lost to the team completely or will be performing at less than full ability.

Many football coaches should wake up to the fact that heavy midweek scrimmaging and contact drills should not be part of tackle football during the regular season.

THE THROWING ARM

Question: I coach a Little League team. My son is a pitcher, and I want to know how to protect his arm. I've seen other kids ruin their arms throwing curveballs or pitching too many innings. Any advice?

Answer: Protecting a pitcher's arm has always been a concern for youth coaches, players, and parents. For expert advice I went to two baseball people who have vast experience both on the field and in the training room.

Larry Starr, the Cincinnati Reds trainer, has seen and worked with many sore arms through the years, too many belonging to youngsters: "I have seen young men who, at twelve and thirteen years old, have been abused and their throwing careers finished. They tore tendons off the bone, disrupted the whole joint, and can't straighten out their arms. At twelve years of age, that's ridiculous. There's no reason it should occur.

"The throwing arm is very delicate," Larry emphasized. "There are two things you have to do: One, warm up properly. If you don't warm up your arm thoroughly, you're going to have problems. And two, don't abuse your arm. Use it intelligently. Don't throw more innings than you should, and don't overthrow before your arm is ready to take it."

As far as the danger signs of an arm injury, Larry said to look for pain and swelling, whether or not the arm hurts in activities outside of baseball. He said: "You know you have problems if your arm hurts when you go to open a door, comb your hair, or just pick up a glass of milk. If doing these types of things hurts, then see a doctor immediately."

Jim Kaat's pitching experience was in the major leagues for twenty-five years and as the Reds' pitching coach. Asked about young arms, curveballs, and arm injuries, Kaat said: "The curveball can do a lot of damage whether you're ten years old or thirty years old. What relates to the amount of damage it will do is how much you're throwing it and who's teaching you how to throw it. I feel as if I could teach a twelve-year-old how to throw a curveball and do it properly, but I'd have to be there with him all the time to make sure he didn't try to throw it too hard or too often."

But unfortunately, of course, few young pitchers, if any,

will ever have someone like Jim Kaat teaching them how to throw a curveball properly. Because of this he offers the following: "While the body is still maturing, the bones growing and the muscles forming, it probably is good advice to stay away from the trick pitches such as the curveball, the knuckleball, and the split-fingered fastball. If you have your mind set on being a pitcher and you're at the Little League level, the best thing you can do for yourself is to learn to throw the fastball and throw it into the strike zone 90 percent of the time."

Jim strongly. emphasized that "if a kid has pain in his shoulder or elbow, rather than continue to throw and think it will go away, he should immediately see a doctor. His arm and his body are telling him something, and that is to stop throwing and have it taken care of."

Kaat covered the prevention of the young pitcher's arm injury very well when he concluded that "steps can be taken to prevent many arm injuries, but discipline is important. Young players must use proper mechanics all the time. They must warm up properly every time out on the field, and they have to take care of their arm and rest it adequately."

OVERTHROWING

Question: I've coached Little League for many years and have always limited the number of innings my pitchers work each week. Too many, however, have continued throwing on their own, either with their friends or fathers, and have come up with sore arms. Isn't this extra practice harmful?

Answer: Although throwing curveballs has always received the most attention, actually the greatest danger to a young pitcher's arm is too much throwing. Now that strict rules to prohibit the number of innings a youngster can throw each week in competition have been instituted and are being enforced, the problem is controlling the number a pitcher throws outside of games.

First of all, a young pitcher should throw very few balls in practice between starts. Too many coaches still have their pitchers throwing during batting practice and working on control when they should be resting their arms. If players thoroughly warm up before each workout and avoid overthrowing, they almost certainly will avoid arm problems.

Overthrowing includes throwing too much, trying to fire too hard on fastballs instead of using a smooth, controlled delivery, and attempting to throw the ball too great a distance. Limiting how much throwing pitchers do away from the mound, making outfielders hit the proper cutoff man whenever possible instead of throwing all the way to the plate, and emphasizing to pitchers control and placement of their pitches instead of just power are all priorities your children's coaches should be enforcing.

Overzealous parents are not always the culprits in overworking a young thrower's arm. They may push their kids too hard, but if you explain the dangers of practicing too much away from organized workouts and games, most will heed the warnings. It's the driven, hungry kids who are most often the hardest to convince. They're striving with good intentions. They want to improve, to strike out all batters, to make the All-Stars, to make it to the big leagues, so they push themselves too hard.

This drive can be difficult to control. After all, young athletes are taught to try their hardest, to work to become the best they can be, to strive to become champions, and to push themselves to accomplish their goals. Keeping all of the above in perspective will be one of your toughest jobs as a parent. Certainly you'll want your kids to perform well and to reach for greatness, but you've got to protect them from injuries when possible.

Pitching is dangerous. Period. Even without curveballs, pitching on any level, including the pros but particularly for youngsters, places a tremendous temptation and stress on a hurler's arm. The temptation to work on new pitches, to throw too hard, and to throw too often all lead to damaged arms and ruined futures for too many youngsters.

Winning is, of course, another problem that leads to unnecessary injury. A coach might use his star pitcher in an important game even when he's hurt or too tired, all within the rules, for instance; or a youngster may stay on the mound while hiding his pain because he wants to tough it out, finish, and win respect and perhaps a championship. The cost of these misjudgments, either misguided or through misdirected heroism, can be devastating. By pushing for one more win, by going one extra inning or even one more pitch, kids can lose everything they've worked for and find themselves out of baseball before even reaching their teens.

Believe me, the proper care and treatment of a young athlete's arm cannot be taken too seriously, and your role as a parent is absolutely essential in ensuring the safety and future opportunities for your children.

WHAT CURVEBALLS REALLY DO

Question: I'm eleven. Do you think I'm too young to throw curveballs? I don't have a very strong arm and my fastball isn't that good, so I throw a lot of curves to make up for it.

Answer: This is one of the most common questions I receive from parents of young baseball players. It's a good sign that kids themselves are beginning to hear and to worry about ruining their arms.

I originally assumed that curveballs, when used in moderation, were safe, but after speaking with a number of experienced doctors, physical therapists, and trainers, I discovered I was wrong. Jack Fadden, head trainer of the Boston Red Sox for many years and Harvard's trainer for the past sixty-six, explained to me the urgency of this problem.

Physically, a young person's elbow is not fully developed until seventeen or eighteen years of age. Children's elbows, when X-rayed, appear to be broken up because the bones are not united. The cracks will eventually fill up with calcium, but it takes many years.

Kids throwing curveballs can cripple themselves. The elbow should not be put under the strain exerted when throwing these pitches. In addition to damaging the bones that are not yet united, it's possible to stretch the ligaments in the elbow as well. These have very little elasticity at any age, and certainly in the preteen years they are not prepared for the work load many young pitchers ask them to carry.

Just throwing a normal fastball before age twelve is enough stress to put on an arm. In fact, unless players are very careful to warm up fully and throw only when they're well rested, they could damage their arm without even throwing a curveball.

There shouldn't be any junkball pitchers in youth baseball. If a pitcher's arm isn't strong enough to overpower hitters, then he or she should either not pitch or begin working on control and hitting spots to get batters out.

If your child's dream is to be a great pitcher and make it to the big leagues someday, then he or she must do the right things now. Working on improving mental concentration, moving the ball around the strike zone, fielding the position well, and learning pitching strategies should be the priorities. Then when the arm matures and your child is taught how to throw breaking balls properly, he or she will be able to combine both mental preparation with more fully developed physical skills to become not just a thrower but a pitcher.

If a coach is allowing a young pitcher to win games by throwing curveballs, then the coach is wrong. This debate has been going on for years now, and youth coaches, parents, and players should understand and accept the real threat to a young pitcher's future in baseball and health in general. It's great to be a star, but not if the price is seriously hurting a youngster's future.

Don't let your kids ruin their careers and their health by throwing curveballs to make All-Star teams. There's no way the results can justify the harm that can be done for a few moments of youth stardom.

7

Conditioning

I've talked to many physical therapists and doctors about how much conditioning young athletes need, and I have to admit I was surprised at their replies. For some reason most of us think kids can run all day and not get tired. But in reality what they commonly do is go at high speed for short spurts and then rest a great deal between intensive activities.

They get tired in sports and other activities because they're forced to run for longer periods of time than they're accustomed to handling without any rest. When kids begin to notice that they lose some speed and skill when they start tiring, make sure you explain to them that this is the reason conditioning is so vital to successful athletes. To play their best they have to work hard to get into shape and stay there.

Youngsters do need to increase their endurance. This can start by trying to run for ten minutes around the field without stopping. Have them take a soccer ball with them and practice dribbling it as they run. They don't have to go too fast, and if they get too tired, they should rest. If they do this three times a week, starting slowly and increasing their time until they've built up to thirty minutes, they'll really feel the results.

Swimming, bicycling, and practicing sports skills will also help to condition them. They can kick a ball and sprint after it and do other ball control drills outside of practice, and they'll find their kicking and stamina improving rapidly in soccer, for instance.

Children have to strengthen their hearts and lungs if they want to play through a game and continue doing well all the way to the final gun. By doing their jogging and other activities, they'll prepare their bodies to work for longer periods of time and be able to play better, longer, and with greater safety, all of which will add up to more fun and success.

As they get older it will become progressively more important to add intelligent, well-supervised conditioning programs that emphasize endurance, flexibility, and strength. Your athletes will be forced to expend as much time as possible away from organized practices and games in weight training, stretching, and running to reach their potential and protect themselves from injury.

Your role is critical in these areas. As you help your kids to understand and accept putting in extra time and effort away from their teams' workouts, they'll be building a foundation of conditioning and creating work habits that will pay off big for them on higher levels of competition. It's not difficult to understand that a well-conditioned athlete can outplay even a more gifted competitor and avoid many of the injuries that occur late in a game or in a season when fatigue begins taking its toll physically and mentally.

Don't abandon your children when they get into their

teens and you no longer feel equipped to practice with them. Continue seeking information for them, push them in their tedious, difficult off-season training, and support their needs when they suddenly feel that all the effort, all the sweat just isn't worth the price they're paying. Your insight and perspective can really help them through the tough times, so remain involved. My parents never even stopped when I retired from professional football at age thirty-four. They're still interested and involved in my tennis, golf, jogging, and volleyball. And I still appreciate and use their guidance as much as ever. Sports truly can provide lifetime influence and strengthen relationships if parents are willing to continue making themselves available and valuable to their children, no matter the respective ages.

STRETCHING

After so many years in sports I still couldn't explain precisely why stretching is so important. I therefore looked for help from others. These were Dr. William Southmayd and Marshall Hoffman and their book, *Sports Health: The Complete Book of Athletic Injuries* (G. P. Putnam's Sons, New York, 1981). What they said, basically, is that stretching cuts down on injuries and helps prevent strains and sprains. Additionally, stretching improves an athlete's speed, balance, agility, strength, and endurance.

It's very important to explain to your boys and girls that proper stretching lengthens the muscles and tendon units. While loosening up, the muscles and tendons fill with blood, which makes them more pliable and less likely to be sprained or strained. The most obvious comparison is with a rubber band. Before they're stretched muscles are like rubber bands pulled taut; they easily can snap or be torn. Good, conscientious stretching makes them loose, able to be handled, stressed, and stretched (lengthened) when necessary.

Emphasize to your children that stretching isn't supposed to be punishment or painful. Relaxing is an important part of proper stretching. If they reach a point where it hurts or is straining them, they should back off, relax, and begin again.

Sports Health gives four rules for stretching that are important for parents to understand and for kids to follow.

1. Always stretch slowly. Never bounce because instead of preventing injuries this can actually create a strain. Each stretch should last between twenty and sixty seconds, and should never be painful.

2. Always stretch for at least fifteen minutes before you exercise or compete. This is important because it takes that long to fill the muscles with blood and stretch out the fibers.

3. Make sure to thoroughly stretch the muscles you'll be using in the exercise or competition you're entering; for example, runners should stretch all of their leg muscles and pitchers should stretch their throwing arm and use small weights to do arm curls, thus warming up their wrists.

4. As you get older you'll need to stretch more, and its importance increases. With aging, muscles become shorter, and they'll have to be worked harder to maintain their flexibility and ability to protect an athlete from injury.

The most important thing you can stress to your kids is that stretching will not only help them become better athletes but will also protect them from many injuries.

Teach them to stretch slowly, properly, and consistently. Once they understand its importance, they'll be more apt to do it correctly and willingly. They'll also know why they're always being told to do it.

GETTING INTO SHAPE (THIRTEEN AND OVER)

There may come a day when your kids will face the dreaded two-a-day practices of preseason football camp. It could be very helpful to their survival and performance if you were in a position to advise them on how best to prepare for this monster. Having been through twenty of them myself, I'll share with you the system I've found the most effective, concentrating on the final phase of their conditioning prior to camp. These workouts can be applied to other sports, too, so if your kids are competing in soccer, track, or basketball, you can show these to them to help their preparation.

The last four to six weeks should be the final thrust in their preparation for the season. They should be doing interval workouts, agility and skill-oriented drills, and some aerobic work such as distance running or bicycling.

There are a variety of ways to do their interval sprint program. They can stride ten 100s with thirty-second rest in between and then finish with ten 40s with half-minute resting periods. If they do this workout, they should start with six of each and add one extra sprint a week until they get to ten.

Another workout I have used for several years that's longer and tougher but has really helped my leg strength, wind, and recovery ability is to start with two 880s, after stretching and warming up. Run each at about three min-

utes and walk a 440 between them. These will build up
the aerobic base and warm the legs for the shorter sprints.
Next, do four 440s, walking a 220 between each. Run
these in one and a half minutes or so, concentrating on
smooth, long strides. Finally, finish with eight 220s with
110-yard walks in between each run. Do these in about
forty-five seconds. This all adds up to three miles of running and another mile or so of walking. This constant
workout will give them strength, deepen their conditioning
base, and allow them to recover from fatigue quickly. These
are all important in preventing injuries and improving the
ability to perform late in games and as the season wears on.

The above workout can be done on Tuesdays and Thurs-
days for one month. During the last two weeks before camp
work can be on shorter distances such as 20-yarders for
starts and quickness and 40- and 60-yard sprints for acceler-
ation and lengthening of stride.

Remember that it's critical to stretch well especially before sprints, and jogging at least an 880 before beginning to
run hard is essential.

On off sprinting days, the athletes should be running
some distance and working on agility drills and the particular skills necessary for their position—such as pass patterns
for receivers, backpedaling for linebackers and defensive
backs, and exploding out of a stance for linemen.

If they do these workouts faithfully and properly, they
should have no problem handling their summer camp.
They might still get a little sore, but they'll recover quickly,
and instead of worrying about making it through preseason
practice they'll be able to concentrate on improving their
skills and playing abilities. They shouldn't try to use camp
to get into shape but rather should show up well conditioned; they'll find themselves far better off. Besides protecting themselves from injuries, particularly muscle pulls

and strains, they'll greatly improve their chances of becoming a far more developed athlete and player by the time the first game comes around.

Finally, your kids shouldn't look at these workouts as survival from preseason camp. They are an important part of their pursuit of excellence in athletics. In addition to the physical benefits they'll receive, the discipline of working out on their own or with friends, away from their coach, will give them more confidence in themselves and in their bodies. I'm sure they'll find the results well worth the extra effort, and they'll thank you for the help and information.

GETTING INTO SHAPE QUICKLY

Question: I think I'm in big trouble, and I'm hoping you can help me somehow. I have only two weeks before preseason football camp, and I'm not in very good shape. Is there anything I can do?

Answer: Ah ha! But what if your kids, like most athletes, put off getting into good enough shape? Here is the final two-week, save-the-day program I developed and specialized in throughout my younger days in football. To minimize the impact of poor training, the first goal should be to eliminate as much of the soreness that muscles will go through during two-a-day practices. Unfortunately, athletes can't get themselves into top condition in two weeks, but what they can do is prepare their bodies for the crunch. They should begin doing the exercises, drills, and conditioning maneuvers their coaches put them through when practices start. They have to do extra repetitions and work hard. They'll be sore, but this will pass after a few days, and then they'll be able to handle the stress with greater tolerance.

It's important that athletes work through their fatigue and soreness because when practices begin they'll want to perform well. Their skills, endurance, strength, speed, and quickness can be severely impaired if they're too tired or too sore to run, catch, block, or jump comfortably.

They should also start working on the specific demands of their position. If they're receivers, they should run patterns. They have to get used to making cuts, running long routes, and reaching for the ball in awkward positions. If they're defensive backs, they can work on backpedaling, starting and stopping quickly, and accelerating after the ball. Linemen should work on their stance, explosion off the ball, and blocking techniques. This work is crucial because their muscles will be better prepared for the unaccustomed work load and their skills will improve in the process. They'll be conditioning themselves for competition and sustained, high level performance.

Running is important, but athletes must be intelligent about their conditioning until camp. They should begin each workout by jogging a mile; then, after some of the calisthenics and exercises they'll be expected to perform, position work should follow before finishing with sprints. Tell them to start with six 100-yard striders, then four 60s at three-quarter speed, six full-speed 40s, and five 20-yard sprints. After a few days they can add a repetition and increase once more during the last week.

Two days prior to practices, they might stretch, jog a few laps, and work on some drills. But, basically, relaxing is the ticket. They will have done everything possible, given the short time they've left themselves, and they'll just have to fight their way through training camp.

Make sure that they learn from the panic they will have

gone through. In following years, starting earlier and building a better foundation of conditioning should be their priorities. The less they have to worry about the fatigue, the more their desire, concentration, and physical talents will shine. Don't let them cheat themselves again. Proper preparation will pay bigger dividends than desperate measures aimed at survival.

THE STATIONARY BICYCLE

Question: I saw your TV show on the stationary bicycle, and I would like to hear your workouts on the bike again. What do you get out of them?

Answer: I really do believe the stationary bicycle is the most underrated piece of exercise equipment around. For some reason it is most commonly thought of as valuable only to older people and those rehabilitating themselves after surgery. Although the bike does, indeed, help those two groups tremendously, it can be a valuable part of any young, aspiring athlete's program too.

For the past eight years I have made the stationary bicycle a big part of my workouts. Besides riding for ten minutes to warm up my legs and body before lifting weights, I also finish with interval training on the bike. These are called thirty-second on and offs. I ride hard, at a high resistance, for thirty seconds, and then I rest for thirty seconds. I repeat this ten times, three days a week. I do my running on alternate days.

The stationary bicycle is great because you can strengthen the legs and work on endurance without the pounding involved in many conditioning exercises such as running and aerobics. I definitely believe in athletes of all ages using the bike. They'll avoid wear and tear on their joints, back, and feet while getting a good workout, whether in a gym or at home, and they'll never have to miss a workout because of inclement weather.

WHY LIFT WEIGHTS?

Questions: I have two sons who will be playing high school sports soon, and I want to know why lifting weights is so important. What does it really do, and why is it being stressed all the time?

Answers: I don't believe a high enough percentage of parents or young athletes truly understand why weight lifting is so crucial to success in today's athletics. Almost everybody accepts the necessity of doing some kind of lifting, but do they understand the benefits, dangers, and why they're putting so much time, sweat, and effort into the activity?

I have to admit that I fell into the ignorant category until about five years ago when the Bengals' strength coach, Kim Wood, sat me down and explained to me what a properly supervised and performed weight-training program can accomplish. I listened because Kim is one of the most respected figures in collegiate and professional sports; he knows his field, and illustrates and backs his points with statistics, studies, and personal experiences.

First, however, picture this: I had lifted through high school, college (both of which were supposed to make me smarter than this), and six years of professional football without really knowing why. I had spent several hours, three times a week, in the weight room, believing I was both dedicated and intelligently going about my business to improve my playing ability. I guess I was there because everybody was doing it, and I didn't want to lose any ground to the competition.

This thinking just isn't good enough. Athletes should know what they're going to receive from their training, not just have the hope they'll either gain an edge or hold off their competition. Knowledge is the greatest motivator, not blind drive or fear.

Besides simply increasing strength, muscle mass, and endurance (making an athlete bigger and stronger for longer), weights provide so much more. They can increase the range of motion, thus improving flexibility, and, in Kim's words, can "enhance the structural integrity of major joints," thus providing protection from injury.

In the simplest terms, weight training is a way of giving athletes more raw material to combine with their natural ability and specific skills. The thinking is that if there are two players who possess equal talent and skills, then the one with greater strength, flexibility, power, and endurance will perform better for longer periods of time and be better able to avoid injury. I've found this to be true as I've watched many athletes actually get bigger, faster, and better under good weight programs. And they've remained healthier too.

Although these concepts sound great, you've got to put them into perspective for your children. Not all athletes will become All-Pros by living in a weight room. There's a limit to what can be gained. You can't create what isn't there, only enhance the ability and physical tools an athlete has been given naturally. Also, overzealousness, improper techniques, and poor training habits can actually lead to injury and have a negative impact on performance.

When explaining the best approach of lifting to your

kids, it is best for them to view it as a means to an end. Weight training alone can't guarantee success on the field, but it can help athletes reach their full potential and move beyond their natural boundaries. To compete in today's sports world they'll have to lift weights, but this training should be only a part of a well rounded program involving flexibility, conditioning, and their own skill development.

When to Start

Question: I've read that some physical therapists and doctors see no problem if athletes as young as ten years old lift weights. They stressed that the exercises must be done correctly, under strict supervision, and using only light weights with high repetitions. What do you think?

Answer: This is a hotly contested subject, one I've debated at length with physical therapists and doctors. There are no concrete answers. "Experts" have opinions, and I've decided that an intelligent, conservative approach is best in this case.

First off, what are the potential gains? Are they really worth the dangers? I don't think so. Weight training involves risk at any age level. Injuries do occur, generally from poor technique or overwork. Certainly the discipline and maturity that a good weight-training program demands are difficult to control and supervise for youngsters.

It's fine to say that using light weights with high repetitions is safe. The problem is controlling the activity. The natural tendency of athletes is to compete, not only with those around them but with themselves as well. This leads to pushing, to attempting record-setting single lifts. Believe me, I know this temptation. I still try to better my personal bests in the bench press even though I know it's far more beneficial and safe to keep going for consistent growth, slowly advancing with weights involving ten successful repetitions.

My concern is that kids will give in and go for big lifts as they gain confidence with lighter weights. This could be particularly dangerous when the calcium and growth plates haven't settled and developed enough. Serious injuries to joints and the neck and back have occurred and are real threats.

Two other major problems with youth weight training are instruction and supervision. How many people are qualified, that is, knowledgeable enough to properly teach workouts? They must be present for each session to ensure that the athletes are continuing to lift correctly and that they are absolutely *not* trying for record-setting heavy lifts.

Besides all of these potential trouble spots, I have to question the positive gains from weight training prior to puberty. Is it really advantageous? Will it improve performance and, more important, prevent injuries, the primary objectives of lifting weights at any age? Again, I think exercises involving a youngster's own body weight—such as push-ups, chin-ups, and sit-ups—are safest and will definitely increase strength and stamina. To risk injury lifting weights without having a substantial potential gain isn't worth it.

There is also the very real threat of burnout. Pushing too hard too young could hurt an athlete's career in the long run. It's a given that weight training is now essential to competition at and beyond the high school level. If youngsters go into those years already mentally tired of the hard work and discipline involved in weight lifting, they might not have the enthusiasm and drive needed to continue improving.

One last concern: A weight-training program without a corresponding flexibility program is ineffective. Strength without flexibility is not practical nor will it prevent injuries or create greater performance. So now you would need complete instruction and supervision for all flexibility and weight-training workouts.

I just don't feel the risks, time involved, and effort justify weight lifting for kids. They should be playing sports for fun and learning how to handle responsibility and pressure. To push them beyond these in hopes of perhaps playing a little better is unwarranted. I'd advise waiting until puberty when they can benefit the most with greater safety.

Recording Workouts

Question: Do you feel it's important to record your workouts when lifting weights?

Answer: Not recording workouts is one of the most critical errors made by young athletes in their weight training. Writing down how much they lift and how many repetitions they complete with each exercise in every workout is absolutely necessary and should not be neglected. You've probably heard that weight lifting is a progressive resistance exercise. This means that as an athlete works out he or she should be attempting to lift heavier weights in a disciplined, controlled progression. For instance, someone bench pressing 150 pounds ten times should add 10 pounds until he or she can once again lift the bar for ten good repetitions at 160 pounds. This weight lifter should then add another 10 pounds and again build up to a full set. This continues as long as the athlete is lifting weights for increased strength and bulk.

135

You'll notice that I didn't mention trying to set personal records for maximum weight, doing one or two repetitions. This type of thinking should be avoided because there's a very real danger of injury, and far more will be gained in strength, flexibility, and endurance through good, consistent sets of ten repetitions with fewer pounds.

Don't let your kids' egos get the best of them; remind them they're pumping iron to improve themselves as athletes and to prevent injuries. There's absolutely no reason to try for one absolute lift. Leave that mentality with the power lifters who compete in their own sport.

Finally, make sure your children record each lift of every workout. This is the only way to chart progress and measure their dedication, improvement, and the true effort they've made.

Machines or Free Weights?

Questions: Do you think athletes should use free weights or machines when lifting? Is one style better or safer?

Answers: I do believe in intelligent, supervised weight training for athletes seeking improved performance and prevention of injuries. I do not endorse weight lifting in pursuit of record, single repetition lifts or ego-fed muscles that do not translate into greater competitiveness and safety.

As far as free weights versus machines, there are no clear-cut, decisive answers. There are advantages and dis-ad-vantages to both, and in truth much can be gained from either or a combination of the two.

Free weights provide a limitless number of exercises, and since they are not attached to a cable or machine, a full motion is possible. Also, specific muscles can be worked on with greater intensity and thoroughness. They're relatively inexpensive when compared to big name machines and are therefore available to more people.

On the negative side, however, skill and technique are much more critical in assuring productivity and safety. Instruction and supervision with a spotter should be considered absolutes, not luxuries or afterthoughts. Overworking, poor form, and fatigue can have a greater impact when lifting free weights. Also, too many kids and adults lift at home alone with their own set of weights. This should not occur; each workout should include either a fellow athlete or someone to help in case of injury or failure in an exercise.

Weight machines such as Nautilus, on the other hand, were created and developed in an effort to ensure greater safety and efficiency. The weights are moved in preset patterns, thus losing some range of motion but eliminating much of the danger of free weights. Changing the weight is as easy as moving a pin up or down a few holes on the stack of attached weights. This saves time and effort. Improvements in variable resistance now allow a greater capacity for a consistent work load throughout a lift, thus actually improving on the free weight workout to a degree. Plus, it is now possible to work more specific groups of muscles.

Ultimately, your decision may be influenced by what you can afford, the availability of machines, and your children's coaches. Understanding the dangers, advantages, shortcomings, and safety of the particular mode of weight training your kids get involved in will mean more than whether they happen to be lifting free weights or working out on machines.

Make sure they lift for the right reasons and make sure they avoid power lifting and body building, which are sports in and of themselves. What they should be after is improving themselves as athletes and then applying their increased strength, flexibility, and endurance to their favorite sports. Your input, support, and involvement are important, particularly when they begin their weight-lifting programs. Keep looking for answers that will improve their results and protect them from unnecessary injury.

Weight Training: How Often?

Question: I'm fourteen and have started lifting weights. How often should I lift?

Answer: There are many workout schedules athletes might follow, but two stand out as the most widely used and recommended. The first and most popular is to lift every other day, such as Monday, Wednesday, and Friday, or Tuesday, Thursday, and Saturday. Here the arms, legs, and back are all emphasized, with a day's rest in between workouts.

The same muscles should not be worked every day. They need rest, and the gains from consecutive workouts will diminish drastically. Consistency is the key. Lifting hard one day, doing extra exercises and repetitions, and then missing a workout defeats the purpose of weight training, which is a gradual increase in strength, flexibility, and endurance. Once a schedule has been selected, keep reminding your child of the importance of sticking with it.

Question: Should I lift weights during the season?

Answer: Athletes should definitely continue lifting weights during the season, but cutting down on their workouts and lifting maybe two times a week instead of three with fewer exercises is important. It's crucial to their health and performance that they maintain the strength and fitness they've achieved during the off-season.

As they play through the schedule, their bodies will get worn down and become more susceptible to injury, and their skills will actually go down unless they keep working out. Most players in the NFL lift on Mondays and Wednesdays during the season, but there are some players who continue with their normal three workouts a week, only scaled down a little.

Ideally, as athletes improve on the field through experience and practice, they should continue to increase or at least maintain their strength, endurance, and conditioning. This will make their play better by the season's end and help protect them from injury.

It's odd that weight lifting during the season has become widely accepted only during the past decade. When you think about it, why should athletes work hard the whole year and then watch their strength diminish during the season by not lifting when they need it most? And, since playoffs and championships are won at the end of the season, it's rather obvious that strength and conditioning are most important during the latter portion of the schedule. Why be weaker during the games that matter most? More important, why should athletes decrease their ability to perform or increase the chances of injury? In-season weight lifting is a must.

Question: I have a sprained wrist so I can't lift weights. How can I keep from losing my strength?

Answer: Lifting around injuries is part of an intelligent, successful weight-training program. It's important to continue every exercise that doesn't involve the injured area.

Our head coach, Forrest Gregg, always told us, "If your

arm is hurt, then lift with your legs. If your leg is hurt, then lift with your arms. If both are hurt, then do neck exercises." What he was telling us was to keep working out or else we were going to lose strength and stamina in our unaffected body parts. Besides maintaining conditioning, this work can actually help heal the injury with greater speed because of the improved circulation and stimulation. Just be sure not to push through an injury by directly working the affected area. This could prolong recovery and increase the severity of the initial injury.

8

Performance

So many parents and kids want to know at early ages whether or not they've got what it takes to be great naturally, or if not, whether they can acquire the size, talents, and skills necessary through hard work, patience, training, and dedication.

Some players are born with a great natural gift and seem to coast effortlessly through level after level of competition. Some even play in the pros for a while on their ability alone. And then there are the players who always seem to perform above their heads and surprise everyone except themselves by starring season after season despite being blessed with less apparent talent. Many keep right on proving themselves all the way to the pros and stick for years.

But for the most part, both of these examples are the exceptions rather than the norm. The truth is that the great, natural players work much harder than people believe, and the hustling, supposedly less gifted athletes have a lot more talent than is often accorded them.

I have to laugh when I hear friends talk about pro players who aren't very good but hang on for years or all the lazy ones who just get by on what they were born with physically. Believe me, every player on every professional team is great, and the ones who appear nonchalant are almost always dedicated, hard workers too. Many, however, fool the press and fans with their personalities and life-styles.

A good example is Cincinnati Bengals All-Pro wide receiver Cris Collinsworth. To the world he's a good-time, free-for-all guy. To listen to him you'd think he partied every night and just showed up to practice on the days he felt like it or happened to wake up. But if you asked anyone on the Cincinnati Bengals, coaches included, everyone would tell you that no one works harder day after day on the field, listens more closely in the meetings, or is hungrier than Cris.

Another athlete who comes to mind is Walter Payton. When I was practicing for the Chicago All-Star game back in 1975, Walter and I were teammates for a three-week period. After each practice I'd stay and punt while almost everybody else headed to the showers, eager to hit Rush Street and some socializing. But not Walter. He was the only guy other than the kickers who stayed out on the field doing extra conditioning and working on some technique or skill he felt he needed to improve.

I marveled at the time at his dedication and at his sheer delight in challenging himself. He was so obviously blessed with speed, quickness, and strength, but he still worked harder than the less talented players who really should have been out there trying somehow to catch up to his abilities. These qualities are what led to Walter Payton's incredible durability and success. He has become one of the greatest running backs in NFL history, not just because he was gifted and lucky but perhaps more important because his work habits protected him from injury and his drive for greatness pushed him through the losing seasons and disappointing performances.

Are great athletes born or made through hard work? In reality, these go hand in hand, but other factors are important too. A strong love for the sport and an intense drive to get better are crucial. Great players enjoy their positions and have an inner need to outperform others and reach the limits of their talents. When this fire dies or even dims through injury, age, or other interests, the players lose their magic. No one can fake it very long in anything; you've got to love what you're doing to do your best.

Dedication off the playing field is also critical. So many great athletes have ended or shortened their careers by drinking, abusing drugs, or just not taking care of themselves. Emphasize this to your kids: They've got to take good care of both their bodies and their minds. If they don't, eventually their physical ability, mental concentration, and zest for life and performance will be destroyed. Once lost, very few ever climb back to the top on or off the field.

Although many different types of athletes make it to the pros, the great ones who stay there the longest are talented and hardworking. They love their sport and are driven to excel. They conscientiously avoid things away from the game that could harm them. These are the ingredients that make All-Pros and Hall of Famers, and no matter what they're involved in, these are the characteristics you should have your children try to acquire.

LACK OF SIZE

Question: Our son is an excellent athlete, but he's small and will probably remain so, given our sizes. Shouldn't we push him into sports other than football or basketball so he'll be able to compete when he's older?

Answer: There is no question that height and weight are in great demand in many sports today, particularly football and basketball. However, the decision to prematurely re-align your children's interests in these sports would be wrong. First of all, there's always the possibility they will mature into big men and women. My parents are only 5 feet 9½ inches and 5 feet 5 inches, yet I am 6 feet 7 inches. Secondly, there has been a movement back to performance rather than raw size and bulk in all the major sports. The qualities of quickness, speed, and toughness are back in vogue. Also, mental discipline, dedication, and intelligence are critical assets that have always carried smaller athletes all the way to the top.

Children should play as many sports as possible, especially those they enjoy. Don't try to protect them from discovering later on that they may lack the size to continue. Their hard work now will be rewarded by the experiences they share with their teammates and their own personal accomplishments. It's also true that if they are forced into some other athletic endeavor sometime in the future because of a lack of size, they'll be better prepared to handle the pressures of competition, and their eye-hand coordination will be further developed. They then can take these skills and savvy to a sport such as soccer, tennis, or track where lack of size might be less of a disadvantage.

Another important thing to remember, and all the more reason to encourage your boys and girls to play sports such as football or basketball in their youth, is that if they do wind up small, the next few years will be the only ones they may have to compete in these sports. These might be their glory seasons when most of the competition will be close to their size, and to take that away from them would be a shame.

I think it would be good for you to sit down with your boys and girls when you fear they may not grow to the height and size they're dreaming of, but be encouraging. Tell them that if they want to continue in football and basketball, there's a chance they may have to lose these sports later on but they should still make the most of today's opportunities and not to worry. Make sure to remind them that there are many athletes who were told in youth sports, in high school, in college, and all the way to the pros that they were too short or too slow or too skinny, but they made it anyway. Hard work, determination, and a little luck all have a way of evening things out in athletics, so it's not always the most physically gifted who make it.

Many college coaches, professional scouts, and front office personnel have told me that they've been too hung up on height, weight, jumping ability, and 40-yard dash times over the past two decades. They've realized there's a whole lot more to an athlete than simply being the perfect physical specimen. They're rapidly moving back to giving their scholarships and big contracts to athletes who are proven winners and performers. Intangibles such as heart, guts, mental discipline, and the love of a sport are being reevaluated as more meaningful than size and speed. So don't discount the possibilities of success later on just because you fear your children's size may become a factor.

Finally, if your kids continue to play those sports that worry you, stick behind them and be positive, not negative forces. The last thing they need are two more doubters, especially their own parents. What will help them most is all the support you can muster, even if the odds do seem stacked against their dreams.

IMPROVING SPEED

Let's face it, there are people who are simply blessed with great speed. They can step out on a track or field and just run past everybody. But that doesn't mean your children can't improve their speed, close the gap, and even start beating these fortunate natural burners.

During my senior year in college I played in an all-star game, and one day after practice I began talking to one of my teammates, Randy White, about trying to get faster. I stood there amazed as he explained to me that in his four years at Maryland he had not only gained forty-five pounds but had also improved his 40-yard dash time by .4 second. I couldn't believe it, but he'd not only gotten bigger and stronger but faster too.

Since that talk and through the years I constantly tried to find ways to cease being a slow wide receiver. Although I still couldn't run as fast as Isaac Curtis or James Lofton, I did make myself a better player by increasing my natural speed.

Your kids can do it, too, but first, they must be patient and consistent in their workouts. They have to build up their endurance by running one to two miles four or five days a week. This will give them a strong conditioning base and allow them to practice longer and do more sprints before becoming fatigued. If they're tired, they're going to be slower, and it's competitive speed that counts, not a 40-yard dash time on a track under perfect conditions.

Second, they must begin a flexibility program; stretching before and after every practice, and continuing throughout the year, is necessary. Improving their flexibility will help protect them from injury, and their quickness will increase as the muscles are better prepared for the stress of making sudden starts, stops, and changes of direction.

The third step should be to get involved in a well-balanced and supervised weight-training program. They need to work their entire bodies and not just the legs. Arms and abdominal muscles are very important in running. They shouldn't simply be lifting for maximum weight. They're seeking power, endurance, and quickness, so using lighter weights with perfect form and higher repetitions is the best formula. The workouts must also be done consistently three days a week.

The final area in which they should concentrate is their running technique. Have your kids work with a track coach. He or she can show them how to improve starts, how to relax while sprinting, the advantages of lengthening their strides, and how to use their arms to greatest advantage.

As their stamina, flexibility, strength, and techniques improve, they'll find themselves running faster. Most important, they'll find it easier to apply this added speed in competition, which is, of course, the goal they should be pursuing.

JUMPING HIGHER

It is possible to improve an athlete's jumping ability, but hard work and patience are absolutes in the process. A close friend of mine, Ron Todd, with whom I'd played high school basketball, had a tryout with the Los Angeles Lakers in 1976. Although he had limitless ability and was six feet one inch, he'd never dunked a basketball and lacked leaping prowess.

Ron was a real gym rat and played hard several hours a day, but despite all the competition he realized he wasn't improving enough to compete with the big boys. He decided to seek help and showed up at my physical therapist's office one day asking how he could improve his quickness and jumping.

Six weeks later, after intensive training that included weight lifting, stretching, resistance bicycle intervals, and running three miles a day with hills in each run, I couldn't believe his incredible improvement. It was funny, but during the first month all he did was complain about sore muscles, being slower on defense, and having lead legs, and he constantly threatened to quit his new program.

But he stuck with it and was dunking easily within two months. He had increased his strength, flexibility, and endurance, which hadn't happened by just playing basketball. Another example of GOING OUTSIDE OF A SPORT TO IMPROVE WITHIN IT.

Make sure your children are guided by a professional in seeking improved leaping ability. Be very careful with their use of certain machines that promise greater jumping. These can place too much stress on the knees and back, and cause injury. Remind them that there's no magic involved here; consistent, intelligent training will guarantee the results they're after.

Also, be sure they work on their entire bodies. Working on the legs alone isn't enough. Try jumping with your arms at your sides; it's difficult, isn't it? The arms, shoulders, and back must all develop equally with the legs if the increase in vertical power is going to be gained.

GETTING OUT OF SLUMPS

Question: I'm playing baseball, and I'm in a bad hitting slump. As a punter, how do you shake off bad games and get out of your slumps?

Answer: Most basic athletic skills, such as hitting, throwing, shooting, and kicking, involve many factors. Proper techniques, timing, mental discipline, and confidence are all crucial for success. Include health, weather conditions, different opponents, and good or bad bounces, and you can see that it doesn't take much for an athlete to lose that little edge temporarily. These down periods are commonly called slumps and are tough to overcome. It takes confidence to excel.

I had a great advantage when I was punting poorly because the Bengals filmed our games and practices, so I could watch the tapes and look for little things I might have been doing wrong. If you, a coach, or a friend has a VCR and camera, you can start taping your kids' play. If you do, you'll have a reference point that might help to discover some flaw in your children's techniques when they begin having a difficult time performing well.

If a VCR is out of the question, then watch your boys and girls very closely so you'll be able to detect problems for them. My dad saved me so many times by noticing something I was doing differently, which my coaches and I had failed to pick up.

When we begin to do poorly in something, the first thing we usually do is get down on ourselves. If your children become mired in a slump, expect them to lose their confidence quickly, to start questioning their abilities, and to become more disillusioned with each setback. These reactions are normal but tough to counteract. Try to remind them that every athlete on every level experiences these frustrating periods when even the most basic plays become seemingly impossible. The key, of course, and what separates the great players from the rest, is getting out of the bad times faster than the competition does.

I've punted since I was eight years old, through Pop Warner, high school, college, and in the NFL, and I had slumps during every single season. Some of them lasted longer than others, but I found that the best and fastest way to get out of one was through hard work and relaxation. These two activities might appear to be at odds, but they're not. Instead of pressing and worrying too much, relaxing and just trying to make easy plays for a while can help. Building confidence through basics is essential. Taking more repetitions and working through a problem patiently but forcefully are the best ways to overcome short-term failure.

I think you'll find, throughout your children's careers in sports, that most of the difficult times will come when there is a lack of mental preparation or concentration, or when they are simply psyching themselves out. If they practice hard, know their team's strategies, and go into games with confidence, usually they'll perform well. The true test of greatness will be in overcoming internal insecurities, momentary lapses of self-confidence, and questions about their ability. Remember, these will pop up from time to time no matter how good they are. I've seen All-Pro receivers drop a couple of passes, and then suddenly they can't seem to catch anything. This usually lasts only until they make a great clutch catch or forget their unfounded worries and go back to performing as everyone knows they can. But for the little while they lose their confidence, no one can help them but themselves because the problem is in their own minds.

When my punting started going sour, I usually wasted a couple of days kicking too much and trying to hit the ball harder and harder. I'd get frustrated, and things would get worse until I'd go back to the basics. I'd start swinging easier and concentrating on doing it smoothly. As my rhythm and confidence returned, I'd start kicking with more power; in no time I would be back on track.

During slumps, players typically begin fighting not only the opponents but themselves, which can be even tougher. If this happens to your kids, have them work harder in practice but concentrate on relaxing in games. They've got to be patient, make corrections, and go into competitive situations with fundamentals and simple execution on their minds. The great plays will follow as their timing, confidence, and a little luck come their way.

COMING OFF THE BENCH

Question: I'm ten years old and playing my first year of sports. I'm not getting in the games that much, but I still want to do well. How should I get ready?

Answer: The first hurdle to performing well as a substitute is to overcome the natural frustration and to keep seeking ways to improve while awaiting an opportunity to shine. Attitude is everything when an athlete is sitting on the bench.

There are several ways to prepare for getting into games and doing well. Physically, athletes must stay warm and ready on the sidelines. They can't just sit around; they must get up and stretch their muscles. Keeping loose by jogging or running in place behind the bench is helpful, and there's no reason to feel self-conscious about it. This activity can prevent injury and ensure that the muscles will be prepared for full-speed action.

If a player is going to handle the ball, he or she should prepare by playing catch with a teammate or tossing it in the air and catching it alone. This will keep the feel in the fingers, give extra confidence, and help focus the eye-hand coordination and skills that will be called upon.

It's vital to stay in the game mentally and not just daydream or cheer on other teammates. Instead, watching what the opponents are doing offensively and defensively, and trying to learn their strengths and weaknesses by studying the starter's performance will prepare a backup for the necessary adjustments to be made upon entering the game.

Additionally, every assignment should be carefully reviewed. A sub must make sure to know exactly what to do on each play. If your child feels confident in what to do, then he or she will be able to simply react instead of having to think. This will eliminate hesitation and allow the physical abilities and skills that have been developed to shine through.

Sure, it's fun to be a starter, but some time on the bench shouldn't be depressing, and the potential growth shouldn't be underestimated. Particularly for young athletes, learning the proper fundamentals, basic strategies, and rules of a sport should be the primary goals.

LEFT-HANDED BASEBALL PLAYERS

Question: I'm playing Little League and I'm left-handed. My coach won't let me play third base or shortstop. I can catch and throw better than the guys playing there, and I'm tired of first base or the outfield. He says only right-handers can play those positions. Is he right?

Answer: I know it's frustrating, but being left-handed will probably hurt your children in baseball. Playing third base, shortstop, second base, or catcher is awkward and difficult for left-handers because of the throwing angles. Some people I've talked to have argued that in youth baseball kids should get to play all positions, and generally I'd agree with them. In fact, I've seen some left-handers playing these positions. But overall I don't think it's a good policy.

Besides being difficult there's a real danger to the throwing arm, particularly at third base. If youngsters charge a bunt, field the ball, and throw quickly to first, they can place too much strain on their arm because of the body position. The same thing is true with backhanding grounders and throwing from shortstop or second base. Also, kids might be better off learning first base, pitching, or the outfield instead of spending so much time and hard work on positions they probably won't get to play after their early playing days are over.

You should take some time to explain these things to your left-handers, at the same time encouraging and reassuring them that they'll still have plenty of opportunities to excel and that they actually have a tremendous advantage at first base and on the mound. By concentrating on the positions they're best suited for, they'll gain more experience and be better prepared to choose those spots on the diamond where they'll be most likely to enjoy their greatest success on the higher levels of their baseball careers.

WRESTLING AND FOOTBALL

Question: I'm a ninth grader. Football is my favorite sport, and I play linebacker. Do you think wrestling would help me make a better football player? If it will, then I'm going for it.

Answer: One of the best ways to become a better football player is to find another sport that complements the physical skills, mental discipline, and conditioning necessary on the gridiron. There's no question that wrestling fits these requirements for a linebacker, and then some.

To more fully explain these advantages, I spoke with Reggie Williams who has played ten seasons as the starting linebacker for the Cincinnati Bengals and competed as an undergraduate on Dartmouth's wrestling team. He is sure that his time on the mat improved his abilities as a football player. Listen to Reggie, and I believe you'll find his response enlightening.

> Wrestling is primarily a man-to-man sport. Agility, quickness, and strength are all necessary to succeed. Just as a linebacker must take on offensive linemen, tight ends, and running backs, a wrestler often has to deal with quicker and stronger opponents. A wrestler learns when to be nimble and avoid unfavorable confrontations and when to be assertive and take advantage of a weakness—important abilities when playing football.
>
> Physically there's no question great gains can be made through wrestling. Quickness and reaction drills really help to develop body control and athleticism. The conditioning necessary to last three periods in competition is great for strength and endurance. An athlete also learns how to use leverage to overcome a size or strength disadvantage, which comes into play all the time in football.

Mentally there is also a tremendous amount to be gained. The discipline of maintaining a certain weight, the grinding workouts, and the personal challenge of winning or losing through your own efforts are invaluable. Plus, it's a tough sport; like football, it teaches survival and aggressiveness.

One thing should be carefully considered, though. To excel and benefit from wrestling, you have to love the sport. You have to enjoy the challenge, the team camaraderie, and the long hours. It's not a sport one can go through at half speed. It takes tremendous dedication, but for any football player, particularly a linebacker, it will prove to be a great help to your development as an athlete, and this will translate into a better performance on the gridiron.

I agree with what Reggie has outlined. Wrestling can help your son become a better football player, but if he doesn't enjoy the sport, he won't get enough out of it for the sweat and time he'll be investing. I do think, however, that if he's interested he should go out for the wrestling team and find out whether he likes it. It's quite possible he'll not only receive great benefits on the football field but find another sport that offers him personal growth, competition, and individual challenges, which are so much a part of wrestling.

SKILLS

Rebounding

Rebounding involves many things. Certainly height and jumping ability can help a player when battling for a carom off the backboard, but there are plenty of ways to offset those advantages. I called Paul Silas, who was a great forward for many seasons with the Boston Celtics and Phoenix Suns. He was not a great jumper or scorer, but when he retired he'd played in the second highest number of games in NBA history (1,253) and was always considered one of the best rebounders in the league at a relatively small six feet seven inches.

He stressed that the real keys to being a solid rebounder are body positioning and timing. When on defense, a player must get a piece of his man and "block him out" on every shot. On offense, fighting for inside position on the man guarding you and constant movement are essentials. He also pointed out that it's not who jumps highest but rather who can reach the ball at the top of their jump the quickest who generally comes down with the rebound. This involves timing and quickness, not just vertical prowess.

Another secret is to always follow your shots. Never put the ball up and just watch the results. So many easy baskets are made by a shooter who, able to tell by the feel of a shot where the ball will bounce on a miss, makes the extra effort to follow it and puts the ball through the hoop on a second try.

Improving the timing of your children's jumps and their positioning can be done with your help away from organized practices. I averaged over twenty-three rebounds as a senior in high school, and my dad was the primary reason. We'd go down to the school, he'd throw the ball off the rim and backboard, and I'd go up to get it. We'd do this over and over again, thousands of times through the years, until I eventually was able to judge all of the strange bounces the ball would take. This helped me immeasurably in games because I could anticipate where the ball would carom off the basket and get there before others. You should do this drill with your kids. It's not tough, but it's very effective.

I'd also emphasize the importance of arm and hand strength. Pulling down rebounds in crowds and holding onto the ball require good power in the shoulders and arms, and strength in the fingers. They can acquire these with fingertip push-ups, gripping and squeezing a tennis ball, and pull-ups, until they're mature enough to begin weight training.

Free Throws

Question: How can I improve my free throw shooting, especially in games where I miss almost every one?

Answer: Successful free throw shooting is a combination of confidence, using proper techniques consistently, being able to relax, and concentrating both in practice and in games. Practicing correctly is important if a player is going to start doing better in games. A player needs to concentrate while shooting every free throw, not just going through the motions. Many teams shoot free throws at the end of their workouts when the players are tired and the quality of execution suffers accordingly. If this is the case with your children's team, have them take their time on each attempt, making each one count and not just shooting the ball and adding up the number of shots until they're finished.

In practice athletes should start developing a rhythm and a routine that they go through before every attempt. The next time they're watching a college or professional game, point out how the great free throw shooters all do the same things prior to shooting every time. Whether it's dribbling the ball a certain number of times (Dennis Johnson of the Boston Celtics dribbles once for every year he's been in the

NBA) or rehearsing the shot without the ball before the referee hands it to them, they follow the identical routine after positioning themselves in the exact spot from which they always shoot.

Your children need to do the same thing. Once they figure out what works best for them, they'll find that the routine will help relax them when they're shooting under pressure in games. The familiarity will allow greater concentration on executing the identical techniques they've been practicing. As the percentages begin picking up in practice, their confidence will grow, and with more success in games their improvement will be steady and a valuable addition to their total game.

Using the Other Hand

Questions: How important do you think it is for my sons to learn to use their other hand to dribble and shoot in basketball? Is this something that is too confusing for youngsters?

Answers: Certainly teaching young boys and girls to use both hands should be done intelligently. Obviously they should feel comfortable and concentrate initially on their dominant, natural side; however, early training can eliminate the awkwardness of forcing a learning process that is very difficult for many players when they're in their teens.

Mastering the basics of shooting and dribbling with either hand is a very individual thing. Confidence and coordination are such key factors when working with kids that to push them too hard, demanding too much too fast, often backfires. They can grow impatient, get embarrassed and frustrated, and quit prematurely.

Common sense should prevail. Some players are more naturally gifted; they'll pick up new, challenging skills with ease. For these, using the other hand will come quickly and add a dimension to their game that will prove invaluable. How many times have you seen Larry Bird toss up some seemingly impossible shot with his left hand when the defender has taken away his right hand? This skill can elevate a player to a higher plane.

Unfortunately, there will be many more kids who simply won't take to using their other hand well at all. For these, patience is critical. Let them try, but do not allow them to get intimidated or down about their inability to use both hands effectively. Instead, have them concentrate on the side with which they're more comfortable. Tell them that as they mature and their skills and fundamentals improve they may be able to add the other hand to their repertoire. But in either case, assure them that it isn't essential to shoot well with both hands to be a great player. It's a bonus they should go for but not one that will ultimately determine their success or failure.

Dunking

Question: I'm a sophomore in high school. I'm six feet six inches, and I'm embarrassed because I can't dunk. What can I do about it?

Answer: Practicing dunking is probably the biggest waste of time and energy for most young players. Instead of worrying about slamming the ball through the hoop with two hands, behind their head, or after a 360-degree turn, they should be working on their jump shots and defense.

Not long ago I was judging a dunking contest in Cincinnati with Oscar Robertson, and we started talking about his incredible career from high school, through college, all the way to the pros, and into the basketball Hall of Fame. Now you have to remember that Oscar, six feet five inches, was one of the greatest players to ever play the game—and *he never once dunked a basketball in a contest*.

My advice to youngsters is to work on the important skills involved in being a good basketball player. Of course they should strengthen their legs and try to jump higher, but they needn't concern themselves so much with dunking. If it comes, fine. But if it doesn't, they can still score just as easily and with greater safety on lay-ups.

Why not work on becoming the very best basketball players they can possibly be? Defense, rebounding, shooting, and passing all win more games and provide many more scholarships than dunking. And believe me, that won't change.

Switch-Hitting

Questions: I'm twelve years old and I'm playing Little League. Do you think I should learn to switch-hit? I bat right-handed and I'm good, but I want to go all the way to the big leagues. Will switch-hitting help me?

Answers: I've received many letters from kids, parents, and youth coaches about switch-hitting. Most of them want to know the pros and cons of having young players learn to hit from both sides of the plate, particularly if they're natural right-handed hitters. At first glance switch-hitting seems to be the way to go. There are many obvious advantages:

160

1. Curveballs break toward the hitter instead of away. Since right-handed pitchers generally outnumber lefties three to one, it helps if a right-handed hitter can switch to the other side of the plate and bat left-handed.

2. Batting left-handed saves the hitter a step on his way to first base. This could translate into additional infield singles, particularly for swift runners.

3. In this day and age of platooning, a switch-hitter will remain in the lineup against all pitchers. This means more playing time, especially in the big leagues.

But even though switch-hitting looks great on the surface, you have to realize that few professional players have had great success doing it. Pete Rose, Mickey Mantle, Maury Wills, and Eddie Murray have benefited, but they are in the minority. For many kids, dividing their time between both sides of the plate might actually hamper development on their natural side. Also, pulling the ball is generally more difficult on the newer side, and there can be a great loss of power.

Wes Parker, a six-time Golden Glove winner at first base with the Los Angeles Dodgers in the 1960s and 1970s, played in their famous switch-hitting infield along with Jim Lefebvre, Maury Wills, and Jim Gilliam. Parker told me that all of them were natural right-handed hitters who added the left side to improve their ability to get on base and to combat the right-handed pitchers' advantages.

On switch-hitting Wes advised: "It's definitely worth trying, particularly at the younger ages. If it feels comfortable and you seem to have the natural talent and ability, it's worth pursuing because there are so many advantages. One of the biggest is that a curveball will generally break in toward you, instead of away from you. No right-hander hitter likes the pitch from a right-hander. It looks like it's coming at your head and then curves over the plate away from you at the last second."

For those children who find they don't have the ability to switch-hit, there is encouraging news. Ty Cobb, Ted Williams, Babe Ruth, Joe DiMaggio, Hank Aaron, and Willie Mays all hit from just one side of the plate and were obviously very successful.

My advice would be that children should try switch-hitting. If it works for them, they should develop the skill as fully as possible. If they can't adjust to both sides of the plate, they'll just have to work that much harder from their natural side. Ultimately, switch-hitting is an individual skill best determined through practice, patience, and an honest appraisal of whether it's beneficial to the hitter trying to conquer it.

Quarterbacking

Question: My son is thirteen and plays quarterback. He has a great deal of athletic talent and a strong arm. His throwing is inconsistent, however. Are there any drills he can do to improve his form and accuracy?

Answer: Being a wide receiver and punter by trade, I was forced to look elsewhere for the answers desired, but I didn't have to look far because Bengals quarterback Kenny Anderson was one of the most efficient passers in NFL history. He has coauthored a book with Jack Clary, *The Art Of Quarterbacking* (Linden Press, 1984), in which he discusses not only the development of physical skills but mental preparation and the importance of leadership in his position.

He suggests several drills that will help your son's throwing. The first, throwing on the run, is becoming increasingly important with all the sprint-outs and moving pockets that are so much in vogue today. Your son should find a partner (it certainly could be you), and these two should set themselves 10 yards apart and run up and down the field throwing to each other. Running from one sideline to the other, two lines apart, across the football field is perfect. The thrower should concentrate on rotating his hips and thus moving his shoulders toward the target.

A strong arm is important, but there are many instances in which a quarterback needs to drop the ball between defenders to complete a pass. This is known as "touch-passing." To develop it, have your child stand 10 to 15 yards in front of some goalposts, with you on the other side. As he moves to the left and right, he should loft the ball over the crossbar into your hands. This will force him to get the ball up softer and drop it to a target instead of just drilling it hard all the time, which can so often lead to incompletions and interceptions.

To develop good throwing technique, have your son place his right knee on the ground and play catch with you. Make sure he throws to the right, center, and left, and he should open his shoulders to the target each time. This is also a good way for him to warm up his arm.

The last drill Kenny recommends is what he calls the "wave and scramble." Stand about 10 yards from your child. Have him drop back to pass and at the clap of your hands he must set himself quickly and throw you the ball. If after he retreats seven steps you haven't signaled him, then he should set up and scramble to the direction you point—back, forward, left, or right. When you clap your hands he should then deliver the ball to you on the move.

There is certainly a lot more to quarterbacking than just having a strong arm and throwing the ball well, but if your son concentrates hard on improving his accuracy and developing a consistent throwing motion, he will be on the right road to success.

Make sure he always warms up thoroughly before throwing any hard or long passes. Just like a pitcher, he must take good care of his arm. Have him wear warm clothing when it's cool, and to avoid soreness and injury he should quit throwing immediately when his arm feels tired.

Catching a Football

Question: How can I learn to catch a football better? I'm only eleven and my hands aren't that big so I drop lots of passes I should hold on to.

Answer: Catching a football well is a skill that can be learned and improved but must be practiced properly, consistently, and often. Definite techniques and fundamentals should be used, no matter what level your children are playing or the size of their hands.

Of course some athletes can catch a ball naturally, but they, too, can get much better by learning to do it properly. For those who have difficulty, the improvement will be immediate and obvious if they make a real effort to catch the ball correctly.

Bruce Coslet, receivers coach and offensive coordinator of the Cincinnati Bengals, played eight seasons as a tight end in the NFL. He has used his personal experience and has also studied All-Pro receivers such as Dwight Clark, Isaac Curtis, Cris Collinsworth, and Dan Ross—all of whom he has coached—to pinpoint little details that many players and coaches may overlook in catching.

He stresses the techniques and fundamentals that professional players work on every day in drills and study in films. Believe me, they do make a big difference. Here are the fundamentals:

1. Always watch the ball all the way into your hands and snap your head down on it until you've gained complete control of it.

2. Use your hands whenever possible. Too many balls bounce off a player's wrist, arm, chest, or shoulder pads.

3. Immediately tuck the ball away safely to avoid drops, being stripped by a defender, or fumbling.

4. Come back and meet the ball whenever possible and address it instead of waiting for the pass to reach you. Not only will this prevent interceptions and passes being broken up, but it will also give a receiver more separation from the defensive player who is ready to make the hit.

5. Use two hands whenever possible.

6. Don't jump or dive for high and low passes unnecessarily. In doing either, a receiver loses body control, which can result in some misses and the loss of valuable time in running with the ball after a catch.

7. Don't try to run before the ball is caught and tucked away.

Here are the techniques:

• *Catching low passes:* The most common error is the receiver's failing to bend his legs and, instead, simply reaching down for the ball. Bending is critical because the fingers should get under the point of the ball, with the hands actually scooping the ball up into the body. If the throw is so low that diving is necessary, the receiver should scoop the ball and at the same time roll over his shoulder with it on the ground. This will prevent the turf knocking the ball loose on impact, thus avoiding an incompletion or fumble.

- *Catching high passes:* A mistake many receivers make is jumping unnecessarily. Keeping the feet on the ground whenever possible will allow more body control on the catch and a better opportunity to run after a completion. The key on any high pass is to get the fingers over the point of the ball, thus stopping its velocity and giving a chance for either a clean catch or a second grab as the ball falls down. Too often receivers fail to stop the momentum of high passes; the ball deflects up into the air, and the defense ends up with a cheap interception.
- *Catching passes behind you:* Do not just reach back and try to make a great catch. The body's momentum moving away from the hands and the speed of the incoming pass will almost always result in a drop. By slowing down and opening the hips to the ball and then reaching back with both hands, a receiver will substantially increase the odds of making a difficult catch.
- *Catching passes in front of you:* Don't try to make a spectacular one-handed catch. Rather, accelerate, try to reach past the ball (do not just short-arm it), and bring it in. If running laterally, try to meet the ball in front rather than as it's flying past the body.

166

Remember, following these fundamentals will help not only wide receivers but also running backs, tight ends, linebackers, and defensive backs as well. They are worth absorbing and putting to work to improve a skill that is such a major part of football.

Punting

Question: My son is a good athlete but probably isn't big enough to play football beyond high school. We've begun fooling around with punting and he's got a strong leg, but he's inconsistent. How did you start kicking, and what advice do you have?

Answer: I started punting when I was eight years old. One day my father and I just started fooling around with it exactly as many fathers and sons do. I can still remember those first few weeks. None of my kickoffs ever left the ground, and my punts spent most of their time going sideways instead of the direction to which I was aiming. Looking back, though, we enjoyed this time together more than when he was hitting ground balls to me or throwing me passes.

As I grew older he couldn't pitch to me, run pass patterns, or play me one-on-one in basketball anymore. But he did continue to be the only person who could help me with my kicking. Everything we learned was by trial and error.

Consequently, only my father knew what I was doing wrong when I kicked poorly. Ironically, he still flew to Cincinnati on occasion to help me out of slumps. The Bengal coaching staff welcomed him with open arms because he always saved me.

I'll try to share with you what we learned through the years.

ALWAYS THROW THE BALL TO YOUR SON. Don't let him just stand there and kick it. Try to bring at least three balls to the field and kick them in both directions, both into and with the wind. Don't just work kicking into your schedule—work around it. Like golf or any other athletic skill, kicking must be practiced consistently and often.

We've found that good punting comes down to these six stages:

- *The Stance*: Stand with your feet parallel so that you can move easily to the left or right for an errant snap. Let your hands hang down between your legs so you are relaxed and low.
- *The Catch*: Catch the ball as cleanly as possible. Move your feet if necessary to keep the ball in front of you.
- *The Steps*: Do not step until you have control of the ball. When moving forward, take small steps and keep on as straight a line as possible.
- *The Drop*: Try to come as close as possible to placing the ball on your foot. Make sure the laces are up and the ball isn't turned too much inside.
- *The Kick*: At contact, your head should be down, eyes on the ball, and your toe should be depressed. Keeping the toe down will give the ball more surface to hit and enable you to "turn the ball over," resulting in more height and distance.
- *The Follow-through*: Try to keep the ball on the foot as long as possible; don't just slap at it. Avoid crossing over your body, and your plant leg should remain on the ground with full extension.

Thinking of all the wonderful hours my father and I have shared kicking the ball, with no one else around, would have been reward enough for both of us. Whether your son ever makes it big in punting is irrelevant. The closeness and time you'll spend together will be worth it.

9

Mental Battles

A couple of years ago I shanked my last punt in a game against the Houston Oilers. Although it hadn't hurt our team much, it did ruin my average, and I was really mad at myself. For two days I moped around complaining about it and worrying that it had cost me the lead for the NFL punting title. My wife, Leslie, didn't know how to comfort me, and I know I tested her patience with my nonstop analyzation and constant reliving of this momentary failure.

This stupid, selfish phase ended on the following Tuesday night when we went to a hospital to visit John Wissel, a high school football player in Cincinnati who had been hurt on the previous Friday night. As I looked down at him, completely immobilized from his spinal injury, preparing himself for surgery that would determine whether he would be paralyzed from the waist down if the operation was successful or totally if it wasn't, I was ashamed. I wondered how I could have wasted so much time and energy over one poor punt when someone like John was so bravely facing an injury that had not just ended his athletic career but possibly would leave him motionless for the rest of his life.

After Leslie and I left John, I went home and started reading some of the letters and questions I'd received since beginning my column. So many of them dealt with handling athletic failure. Some were from parents wondering how to comfort their sons or daughters who had made a play or struck out with the bases loaded to cost their team a game. Others were from young athletes themselves asking if they should quit because they had let their team down or because they weren't performing to their potential.

I've never answered most of these in my column because, like Leslie, I didn't know how to comfort those who were disappointed, embarrassed, or mad at failing themselves or their teammates.

I do know now, however. When your children are upset at a performance or are having trouble handling a tough loss, tell them to think of John Wissel lying in his hospital bed in Ohio. Please remind them that when they leave a game healthy, they've won, no matter how badly they might have played. They'll have another chance to go out there and do better. They'll still be able to practice and improve and, above all else, will still be whole.

Don't allow them to get hung up on averages or championships to the point that they lose track of the place sports should take in their lives. When they leave a game, they should get ready for the next one and be thankful that they'll be healthy enough to have another opportunity. THEY SHOULD BE APPRECIATIVE OF THEIR TALENTS AND BE GRATEFUL FOR EVERY CHANCE TO DISPLAY THEM. When they're really feeling down, have them go out and run a lap, feeling the strength in their legs, shake their arms, and wipe the sweat off their faces. When they finish, they should remember John Wissel.

And feel lucky.

MAINTAINING ELIGIBILITY

Question: Do you agree with new legislation such as the "no pass, no play" rule in Texas?

Answer: Sadly, I've known a great many athletes through the years who were totally unprepared for life without sports. Society suddenly rejected them because they weren't needed any longer for entertainment; they were labeled losers when they couldn't make a smooth transition into the real world. This is all wrong. All through their lives these men and women were cheated by school officials, coaches, and even their parents. Most kids are going to try to get away with as much as they can, especially in the classroom, and the results are the responsibility of those who are supposed to be guiding and influencing them.

If athletes can't make good grades, they should be forced to pay the price. Not just in words but through action. Texas, along with other states, has attempted to do something about the overly competitive, immoral, and excel-at-all-costs nature of much of today's high school sports.

All athletes should have to maintain passing grades. Although athletics can be a positive influence and are great for many personal goals and achievements, kids are still in school to learn, not to score touchdowns or dunk basketballs. They should be preparing for the future, not just playing games.

The impact in Texas has been substantial. Many gifted

athletes have been denied the opportunity to play because of failing grades, and in the long run this is the best thing that could happen to them. If they continued to be pushed through high school without the proper foundations in reading and writing, they would be in big trouble. Even if they receive an athletic scholarship and squeeze through a few years as undergraduates and their eligibility is used up, they'll have no options unless they get lucky once again and get a professional contract. But sadder still, if they do manage to earn a living as a pro for a few years, they'll be even further behind when they finally cease being athletes and become normal citizens.

There is no question some athletes are still slipping through with unearned marks and easy classes, but recent legislation has taken a giant step in the right direction. SOCIETY DOESN'T OWE GIFTED ATHLETES "FREE RIDES" TO COLLEGE; IT OWES THEM AN OPPORTUNITY TO SUCCEED AS HUMAN BEINGS. Sports cannot guarantee this; in fact, they've been proven to retard an individual's personal development if not kept in a balanced perspective.

If a firm, new direction that establishes sports as extracurricular activities is not followed, I fear our entire athletic system will soon topple. School officials are the ones who must take a stand; after all, it's the schools who are offering the activities in the first place. If athletics become more important to students than their marks, they should be denied the privilege of playing and representing themselves and their schools on the playing field.

The decision should not be made by athletes. It's a job for parents, principals, coaches, and the athletic directors of our schools. Unless these officials and you start living up to your professions and your responsibilities, too many kids are going to cheat themselves and society of the individuals they could become.

Don't let this happen to your children. If they're not being pushed hard enough by the system, its coaches, teachers, and administration, then it's up to you to ensure their future opportunities both on and off the field. INSIST THAT CHILDREN DEVELOP FUNDAMENTAL STUDY SKILLS AND LEARNING HABITS FROM THE DAY THEY ENTER SCHOOL. TO MISS THIS RESPONSIBILITY IS TO FAIL YOUR KIDS IN A CRUCIAL AREA, WHICH WILL ALMOST SURELY COST THEM HEAVILY THE REST OF THEIR LIVES.

PLAYING AND STUDYING

Question: Do you have any special hints you could give students who are very active in sports and trying to maintain a good scholastic record at the same time?

Answer: The first and most important step in becoming and remaining a good student athlete is to accept sports for what they were intended to be: extracurricular activities.

Kids don't go to school to play football, be a cheerleader, or play an instrument in the marching band. They go to learn and to improve their minds. All other activities are bonuses. They are available to help round out individuals.

Aside from their obvious physical benefits, athletics are valuable for the lessons they teach that can be applied throughout life. However, teamwork, dedication, and discipline don't add up to much if our children aren't educated and qualified for college or a career.

Besides simply keeping athletics in perspective, there are some practical tips that might help your children to succeed as student-athletes. First, encourage them to budget their time. With all the hours of practice, athletes can be handicapped in competition with their classmates. It's tough to go home after long, exhausting workouts and hit the books, and therefore using free time and energies wisely is very important. I always tried to have a study hall during school hours and then divided the remainder of my schoolwork before and after dinner.

It's crucial, too, for athletes to avoid falling behind in their studies. Again, a lack of time and energy will make it difficult to cram or catch up when papers and exams start cropping up. Your child should apply the teamwork concept he or she has learned in sports, calling on friends, teachers, and you, if necessary, to help them succeed academically. Leaning on teammates and asking a coach for extra work on techniques or skills are encouraged in athletics; they should also be used by athletes when they need others to reach their goals in other areas of their lives.

Sports should not interfere with an education, but at the same time studies do not have to force a student to reduce his or her athletic dreams and accomplishments. A balance can be found; it's up to you to guide and maintain this all-important combination.

NERVOUSNESS

Overcoming nervousness is a big part of sports. Like many youngsters, I still have problems playing well at the beginning of games. Whether it is a volleyball tournament on the sand out in California or my first punt against the Pittsburgh Steelers in Riverfront Stadium, it has always taken me a while to feel comfortable.

One thing you should emphasize to your children is that nervousness is normal. Almost every athlete I've known, in all sports and at every level, has been a little tight before games. In fact, you'll find that when athletes stop feeling butterflies in their stomachs, they seldom have outstanding performances.

Different players find a variety of ways to help themselves relax. We had an All-Pro player on the Bengals who threw up before every game and continued to do so throughout his career. Some athletes read the Bible or other books to take their minds off the upcoming game. Others study their playbooks and scouting reports, even though they probably know them frontward and backward. They just believe that the more prepared they are, the less they have to worry about making mistakes.

I think the greatest error I made, early in my career, was to "save" myself for the game during warm-ups. I tended to put forth very little effort in the exercises and patterns I ran before the games. Because of this I would become progressively more tired as the tension mounted and I resisted releasing it. Now, however, I really try to explode during warm-ups. I've discovered that instead of making me tired, running hard relaxes me and prepares me better to go full speed on the first play.

Nervousness is not necessarily based on personality or confidence. Because the body is anticipating rigorous physical activity, its chemistry changes to aid performance. Medically this is termed the "fight or flight" syndrome.

Before a game there are chemical, physical, and psychological adjustments your children's minds and bodies will make naturally to protect and prepare them for a heightened performance level. This is why some athletes are able to make incredible plays in games that they couldn't make in practice. On the other hand, some others may play worse if they don't adjust to the tension and stress they're facing.

Tell your children not to worry about being nervous. It's a universal and natural reaction. Instead, they should concentrate on relaxing, warming up aggressively, and applying the skills they've been practicing so hard in preparation for their games.

MENTAL PREPARATION

The first step in mental preparation is actually physical. Your children must practice hard to learn the correct adjustments and techniques they'll use in the games. After they receive their assignments and strategies for an upcoming opponent, they should concentrate on applying as much intensity and full-speed preparation as possible during the week.

Step two is to know each assignment—not just the basic skill or task but the proper adjustment against different defenses or offenses. For instance, receivers should rehearse in their minds what they should do against a bump-and-run cornerback; guards should know what happens to the blocking scheme if a linebacker or safety blitzes in football.

In basketball, strategies of adjusting to man-to-man or zone defenses should be practiced mentally. And in baseball, players should plan where they'll throw the ball with runners at second and third, with one out and a two-run lead. These situations are endless, and the more they're rehearsed, the better an athlete will react when faced with the play in competition.

Through the years I've seen too many players fail because they didn't practice hard enough or know their plays well enough. When they got into game situations, instead of just reacting, using their talent and the skills they had developed, they were unsure, hesitated, and were unable to react at full speed.

Don't allow this to happen to your kids. Games should be their opportunity to showcase all of their dedication and ability. They should prepare thoroughly before taking the field for games. If it means staying after practice to work on some individual techniques, spending extra time with coaches going over strategies, or hitting their playbook every night, they must do it. The rewards are worth the extra effort, and they'll be creating work habits that will aid them in whatever they do after their competitive sports careers are over.

CONCENTRATION AND DISCIPLINE

Question: In many of your articles you cover subjects concerning physical development—weight lifting, conditioning, and stretching seem to be the most common. Isn't mental preparation just as important for an athlete to reach his or her potential?

Answer: There's no question that athletes must develop both physically and mentally to reach and remain at the top of their abilities in any sport. In fact, many less physically gifted athletes make it because of their mental toughness, while at the same time many great "natural" athletes fail because of their lack of mental development and discipline.

The Los Angeles Dodgers Wes Parker was well known for his intense mental preparation. During his career he was an outspoken advocate of *Psycho-Cybernetics*, a book written by Dr. Maxwell Maltz, and took what he read there and molded it for his own personality and needs. Said Wes:

I reached a point when I felt I had taken my physical talents just about as far as I could. I realized that in order to continue improving, to reach a higher level of performance, I needed to work on my mental development. I began to spend nearly as much time on my mind as my body, and the results were significant.

There were two major areas I worked on hardest. The first was concentration. I realized that I needed to bear down and really concentrate on every pitch and fielding play, not just when I was going good or felt like it. This discipline raised my average and made me an even better infielder. Second, I started increasing my positive thoughts. I visualized knocking in a game-winning hit or making a great play as often as possible.

When negative thoughts or doubts popped into my head, I would force myself to think of the good things I'd already accomplished and other goals I was pursuing. This helped my confidence and kept me up after bad games, and I played at a more consistent, higher level through both good and bad periods throughout our long season in the major leagues.

It's my belief that by developing both their mental and physical powers as fully as possible, athletes will go further and get the most out of their talents and potential.

There is too much emphasis being placed on getting bigger, stronger, and faster in today's sports. Young athletes should also be taught and made to understand the value and importance of training their minds and applying these techniques both on and off the field.

Through the years I have watched many players come and go through the NFL. Generally the ones who stayed the longest and accomplished the most were very disciplined individuals who had great knowledge of their positions and the game of football on the whole. They continued developing their mental abilities as their natural physical

179

gifts were declining. In this way they not only lengthened their careers but became fuller, better players.

For young athletes, the sooner they can combine their physical talents with an ever-growing mental maturity, the better they'll perform and the closer they'll come to reaching their full potential. You should make sure your kids don't simply concentrate on hard workouts. but that they also start thinking, listening, and reading to reach their full potential.

THE MARTIAL ARTS

Question: I'm thirteen, and I want to start taking karate classes because I've read that it has helped some really great athletes, but my parents don't think it'll do me any good. Aren't they wrong?

Answer: I definitely believe that the martial arts can be tremendously helpful to athletes. I'm involved in Tae Kwon Do, having taken private lessons, and I've found the classes exciting, satisfying, and helpful. My instructor, Jon Wiedenman, has had a great influence and impact on my life. I've always pushed myself and other athletes to go outside their main sports to improve their conditioning, coordination, and performance, and there's no question in my mind that martial arts can do these things for any athlete.

There's so much more to the martial arts than just fighting, kicking, and defending yourself. I started Tae Kwon Do with three specific goals in mind. The first was to improve my flexibility. Stretching is a vital part of every workout in karate. Before learning the intricate footwork and kicks, each student must be able to perform the drills physically. This takes an intense flexibility program that usually consumes up to a third of each session. All the major muscles and joints are worked on—the hamstrings, groins, back, knees, neck, hips, and even shoulders and arms. It not only strengthens the muscles but provides a good foundation of exercises for warming up for any sport and leads to better endurance and performance, and helps to prevent injury.

My second goal was to toughen up mentally and physically. The basic forms and drills are difficult, tiring, and take great concentration and practice to learn and perfect. Discipline is a major issue in martial arts, and the lessons learned and the confidence gained have great carryover effect in other sports and life. It's amazing how much inner strength we all have that is never tapped because we're not pushed hard enough or challenged to our limits. For any athlete, learning to cope with and overcome fatigue and fear of failure are essential to success and personal satisfaction. Karate definitely provides the opportunity to test your own reserves and to set new standards of endurance and performance.

The final goal I wanted to reach through my martial arts training was the ability to focus totally on what I was attempting to accomplish. The perfection of form and repetition—so much a part of Tae Kwon Do—has taught me to bring all of my physical skills together to perform the task I am attempting. This type of focus is critical to a baseball hitter, a basketball player shooting a jump shot, or in my case, a football punter. It must be obtained through training; it can't be gained through practice in a sport alone. There are many ways for an athlete to learn the ability to centralize all of his or her resources on the task at hand, but I've found none better than the philosophy and teachings that are so basic to all martial arts.

Many outstanding athletes, including Kareem Abdul Jabbar of the Los Angeles Lakers and Andre Tippett of the New England Patriots, deeply believe in their martial arts training. There is no question that their dedication and willingness to go outside their particular sport have been at least partially responsible for their great success.

If you're concerned about your children becoming involved in these activities, talk to an instructor and observe a class and all of the discipline, concentration, and training involved. I'm confident you'll find the atmosphere a healthy and inspiring one.

HITTING THE PLAYBOOK

Question: My son plays football. I've tried to explain to him the importance of studying his playbook, but all he really wants to do is play. Can you help?

Answer: Every year there are players who don't make NFL teams simply because they don't spend enough time learning their plays. They have all the physical talent necessary to block, tackle, catch, and run in the pros, but because they're unsure of their assignments, they make mistakes or play cautiously, with their performance suffering accordingly. On the other hand, there are less physically gifted athletes who do make teams because they are knowledgeable, smart on their feet, and consistently get the job done. They are prepared and understand their plays and assignments.

The same thing happens on high school and college levels. Talented players sit on the bench behind guys who are more dependable and sure about their plays. These bench warmers simply don't listen carefully enough to the coaches, they don't study their game plans on their own, and they're irresponsible in carrying out their positions on the field.

Make sure your children don't make this mistake. It doesn't matter how dedicated they are to running and lifting weights, or how aggressively they might play; if they're unsure of what they're doing, then they'll never reach their full potential. Remind them that they have a responsibility to carry out their part of a play. If they make an assignment error, they will let down their team just as much as if they'd booted a ground ball, missed a tackle, or blown a lay-up.

Your children should know their positions and assignments, and rehearse all of the adjustments they may have to make in a game. These may be according to an opponent's defense, offense, or personnel. If they study their plays hard and prepare themselves, they won't have to make decisions on the move but will be able to react and play because they've practiced it. They'll not only play better individually but also contribute more to their team, and their consistency and level of performance will dramatically improve.

PLAYING ON LOSING TEAMS

Questions: Our son is eleven. He's playing baseball, and his team hasn't won a game this year. Last year his soccer team won only two, and his football team wasn't much better. Won't all of this losing affect his attitude, and can you think of any way we can help him?

Answers: One year when I was in Little League I was on a terrible team. We lost several of our early games by so many runs that the umpires called the contests because we simply had no chance. I can still feel the helplessness and humiliation, but although we didn't have much talent, we did have a good coach who continued to teach us patiently how to catch, throw, run the bases, and swing a bat. As the weeks passed we started improving, and by the end of the year we were actually winning some games.

I can remember enjoying the excitement of our first win, but to be honest, I enjoyed myself almost equally throughout the season. Getting to wear my uniform, playing in front of people, making a catch here and there, and getting on base were enough to keep me excited and interested. The score of the game was really incidental.

Obviously it's fun winning at any level of athletics, but maybe it's not as important to kids as you might think. Too many of us assume that going out for ice cream or pizzas would be a lot more fun after a victory than after another loss for them. But in either case, win or lose, kids in general will partake of the festivities if they're offered. And this is my major point. Most children really aren't that hung up on winning or losing. It's adults, both as coaches and parents, who influence young athletes' reactions to victories and defeats, and can affect their feelings either way.

I've talked to plenty of youngsters on losing teams, and they assured me they were still having fun. After all, the seasons aren't that long, and with such a variety of sports, they figured they'd have a good shot at being on a winner in a couple of months. Kids simply don't carry losses with them for very long, even for championships. They're off and running after new adventures long before their parents or coaches get over a disappointing game.

As your children get older and begin to make conscious choices with regard to use of their time, playing on a losing team might ruin their enjoyment of a sport and might influence them to direct their energies into another sport or another activity altogether. But for now they shouldn't be worrying about batting averages and championships as much as just having a good time.

It's your job to make sure they're gracious in both victory and defeat. And although it's difficult, you must avoid allowing your attitude and drive for winning to put pressure on your boys and girls. Forget about their teams' records. Laugh off the losses and celebrate the victories. Buy them the same size ice cream cone after the game, whichever way it went, and talk about the game and how they played, not the outcome.

A FRUSTRATED SUBSTITUTE

Question: I'm the sixth man on my high school basketball team, just like last year. I want to be a starter, but my coach keeps telling me I help the team more by coming off the bench. What can I do about it?

Answer: It's easy to understand a substitute's frustration. Every athlete wants to be a starter—there's more prestige and publicity, and anyone who's competitive wants to be out on the field as much as possible. While there's nothing wrong with a child's disappointment at being on the bench, individual goals and feelings shouldn't get in the way of performance or hurt the team.

Many athletes were tremendously successful coming off the bench and eventually became starters. I can remember Donnie Shell being a special team's star long before he became a perennial All-Pro strong safety for the Pittsburgh Steelers. John Havlicek was a superb sixth man for the

Boston Celtics for years before he broke into the starting lineup—and of course blossomed into an All-Star and Hall of Famer.

Your child might be a substitute for some time. Being hung up on starting might affect your child's drive to excel, but don't let him or her stop working hard and improving. If a coach feels the team is stronger with your child coming off the bench, he or she has to accept it and play that role to the best of his or her ability. Strong winning teams rely on talented substitutes. If they're as good as the starters on the squad, they can be extremely valuable upon entering a game. Make sure your child takes pride in this and looks forward to the idea of coming into a tight situation and saving the day, perhaps emerging as a hero.

The best thing you can do for children on the bench is encourage them and make them appreciate their importance to the team. Also, they must understand they have to continue working hard and developing their skills for the time when their chance comes. If their frustrations start poisoning their attitude, they'll stop improving physically and the sport will no longer be fun. Don't let this happen. Push them, console them, do everything possible to teach them that patience, hard work, and contributing to a team in any way they can are what team sports and life are all about.

PLAYING BEHIND AN INJURED STARTER

Question: My boy sits on the bench after working hard all week while this coach starts and plays another kid who has been nursing a pulled muscle for over a month. Don't you think that the one who practices should play in the games?

Answer: On the surface there appears no question that an athlete who has been practicing, sweating, and preparing every day should be the starter when game time rolls around. He or she deserves the chance to prove his or her abilities on the field, and the team should have the healthiest, most readied player performing.

The problem is, however, that a coach must determine whether or not the physical skills, experience, and talents of the injured player are enough to offset all of the missed practices. The coach must decide if that player, at even less than 100 percent, is still more valuable to the team than a better prepared backup who has been working hard and waiting for an opportunity.

Having been in the substitute's position several times in college and professional football, I know the frustration that can ensue. I can also relate to an athlete's or parent's great desire to try to knock some sense into the coach. This isn't always the best course, however, and your interference could actually hurt your child's chances of playing. What you must do is encourage your athlete to continue working hard, preparing for the possibility that the coach will alter his or her philosophy.

Too many coaches stick with their starters, even playing those who are hurt when they'd be far better off putting in healthy backups who have practiced, are hungry, and deserve their chance. The injured players, if given a week or two of complete rest and rehabilitation, might avoid lingering problems and return to action quicker and at full speed, and the substitutes who have been practicing would get their shot and their rewards for dedication. Then, after a short time, the coach would have both the original starters and some seasoned backups, making a stronger, deeper team.

All of this is logical and obvious to outsiders. But to a coach facing an upcoming game the tendency is often to continue using the players who have earned positions and shown superiority over their teammates earlier in the season.

I can remember starting games, performing well, practicing with the first string for the entire week following, and then watching from the sidelines with anger and frustration as the player I had replaced hobbled through the first half of the game doing nothing. As you can see, what you and your children might go through will not be unique. It's an unfortunate but common trait of organized sports.

Earlier I emphasized the importance of keeping up your child's spirits, encouraging him or her to hang in there and to continue working with the hope that he or she would get a chance. Naturally I can't promise that things will break this way, but all of you should try to make the most of this character-building opportunity. Remember that sports, like life, aren't always fair, that athletics are supposed to teach a person more than just fundamental physical skills.

This may not be the easiest medicine to swallow, but you don't have many other options. Getting through the season might be tough, although your child's chance could appear overnight. Whichever way it goes, it is most important to make sure your athlete continues improving his or her skills, preparing to help the team even if it's only by practicing hard and ensuring that personal growth isn't discarded through bitterness.

This will definitely be one of the most frustrating problems an athlete or parent can go through, so it's even more important that you're prepared to handle this explosive situation and help your child through it wisely.

A SUBSTITUTE'S REWARDS

Question: Our son is a good athlete but has never really gotten to play much. He puts in a great deal of time and energy although he knows he'll never be a star, but he keeps practicing and sitting on the bench anyway. We don't want to discourage him, but don't you think he should get involved in something in which he might be more successful?

Answer: There is so much more to athletics than being a star. Sure it's great to receive the awards and fame that go with stardom, but they're just bonuses, not the only reasons for playing. Whatever happened to things like enjoying the competition, sharing the camaraderie among teammates, and developing discipline and dedication? Believe it or not, sports were not originally offered and encouraged by schools in order to win games and make stars; they were viewed as a valuable extension of a student's education and personal development.

Somewhere along the line, probably because of television coverage and large professional contracts, too many of us have lost track of these priorities. There's nothing wrong with being a substitute. There's nothing wrong with working hard, enjoying a sport, and watching your teammates make the headlines. Instead of discouraging less talented athletes, parents should be proud of their dedication and selflessness. After all, isn't genuine personal satisfaction far longer lasting and meaningful than fame or superficial rewards?

If your children are backups, you might wonder if they should quit and find something else in which they'd be more successful. I think the work habits and persistence they'll learn, with little reward beyond what they share with their team, will make them very successful. These are irreplaceable and will help them throughout their lives, far more than trophies and press clippings.

Most of the publicity does go to the great natural players who just seem to step on the field and excel immediately. But actually these are the exception rather than the rule. In truth, most players either sit on the bench and work their way up to a starting position or remain substitutes throughout their careers.

In fact, the entire competitive system was set up and works in this manner: The majority of players move up level by level. They start on the freshman team in high school or college, move up to the sophomore squad, then the junior varsity, and finally the varsity, many waiting until their senior year to make it. This gradual climb allows for more participation by more students and gives them time to develop physically and mentally until they are prepared for and rewarded by making the varsity team.

Sports, like life, are unpredictable. Your son or daughter may never leave the bench, but who's to say that he or she's not just a late bloomer and may yet become a star. He or she might get an opportunity because someone starting gets hurt or plays poorly, or simply because the coach thinks a reserve has earned a chance. In any case, you should be encouraging your kids to continue their quest and be thankful that they have the drive and guts to keep playing, despite discouragement and a lack of success on the field.

BEING RECRUITED

Having a child who's a gifted athlete will have its price, particularly during their senior year in high school. College recruiters will begin to intensify their efforts, and these salesmen, disguised as coaches, will be pressuring you and your offspring to sign a letter of intent. In all of the hoopla, excitement, and competition, the difficulty and impact of this entire process are generally ignored or overlooked.

Having been through this experience as a recruit for my alma mater for many years and having listened to countless stories and experiences from other players, I know that very few teenagers or their parents are prepared to select an institution without a great deal of anguish and indecision. After all, this is a decision not only affecting the playing career of athletes but their development as individuals, their education and, ultimately, the course of their lives.

Before accepting any campus visits or committing to anything, review the NCAA rules and regulations on recruitment. Don't violate any of these. If a coach or an alumnus offers you or your child anything illegal, do not accept. In fact, forget the school. The chances are they're offering other prospects similar gifts. They'll eventually get caught, and your son or daughter could lose a chance to go to a bowl game or be on national television because the team will be on probation.

When your children visit a campus, make sure they get away from coaches and players and spend some time just wandering around the school on their own. They should talk to students and athletes encountered by chance. I was never comfortable on a tight itinerary because I always felt I was talking only to certain people who were telling me certain things. Getting an independent feel for the environment is very important, giving a better idea whether four or five years would be enjoyable there. Also, if you know someone who is already attending, all of you should talk to that person and see how he or she likes it.

It's very important that a high school senior consider a

school's other factors besides its athletics. Coaches leave and philosophies change, and an athlete may suddenly find himself sitting on the bench because his talents are no longer desired. The object is to find an institution that your child will enjoy socially, benefit from scholastically, and be comfortable attending with or without athletics.

Remember, your child might get injured, might be unlucky or find himself playing behind an O. J. Simpson or Magic Johnson, or might decide that sports are less important than studies or outside interests. In other words, a decision based on a coach, a pro career, or a team's great winning tradition is not a sound decision.

Some athletic considerations might concern who is already playing at the school, what other players are being recruited in the same position, and whether the coaching staff is planning to use them. Be wary of coaches who guarantee a starting position to a freshman or who bad-mouth the competition. Also, take your time and commit as late as possible so that you'll have a better idea who else has been signed and whether your child will be given a fair shot at starting.

No matter which school is selected, your child will have second thoughts and doubts. That's why it's so important to consider priorities carefully and find a school that appears to offer fulfillment. Athletics are too full of disappointment, bad luck, injuries, and unrealized potential. I would therefore emphasize academics, extracurricular resources, and a campus that feels right. If your child makes All-American, so much the better, but make sure you know about educational prospects and campus life before signing that letter of intent.

NOT BEING RECRUITED

Question: I've started for three years now at defensive end for my high school. I guess because I'm only six feet tall nobody's recruiting me, but I want to keep playing. Aren't there ways to get colleges interested in me, or am I finished?

Answer: There are a great number of outstanding high school athletes who aren't recruited by colleges or offered scholarships. Some are too small while others lack talent as defined by statistics, such as 40-yard dash time, jumping ability, or bench press strength. Still others have simply been playing out of position, in the wrong system to showcase their skills, or at schools that are so small they're not heard about or scouted.

You can have tremendous impact in this area. Too many athletes get frustrated because no one shows interest in them. They not only suffer mentally but allow their performances to decline because they're down. There doesn't seem to be much point in continuing to push hard if they're not going to get an opportunity to play at a higher level of competition.

Don't allow this to happen to your kids. I can't emphasize enough how many players have been discovered by recruiters who had gone to a game to scout someone else but left impressed by some unknown player. This is why it's so critical that high school seniors keep their hopes alive and play hard instead of just going through the motions and feeling sorry for themselves. They truly can be discovered when they least expect it, and it's important that they have good films to send to schools later on if it becomes necessary.

Although big schools may not be going after your child, many other possibilities are available. The coach may have a friend at a school who will come and take a look on the strength of a personal recommendation. Or an athlete could have a friend or ex-teammate already on scholarship somewhere who'll put in a good word that could result in an opportunity. Many players are signed late, after colleges fail to land the blue-chippers they were after, so giving up prematurely is a mistake.

There are also plenty of small colleges that may not give full rides but can provide some aid. Grades are critical in many of these institutions, so a good student-athlete has a far better shot than a player with poor grades. Because these schools don't have big recruiting budgets, they rely on heresay and players calling them up and sending films for their review. Don't be shy about praising your child's ability or feel uncomfortable approaching these colleges. They need this interaction.

Another oft-traveled route is through junior college. This allows two more years to grow physically, mature mentally, and improve the level of performance. Just as important, a junior college can give an athlete an opportunity to play a different position, possibly one he or she is better suited for, or to perform under a different coaching philosophy that may create better opportunities for success.

If after trying all of these things nothing has popped up, however, your kids can still try out as walk-ons. As an analyst for ESPN's weekly college football games, I've been amazed at how many players have walked on, made teams, become starters, and even made All-American in major programs. At Nebraska alone there were thirteen walk-ons in 1986, many of whom had earned full scholarships and several of whom had become starters.

Don't let your high school athletes get too discouraged too quickly. Naturally not being wanted is an ego-deflating experience, but if they want to play badly enough, the chances are that they'll be able to find a vehicle. They may have to hustle, be creative, and settle for less than their full dream, at least temporarily, but they can find a way. Help them. Think of contacts, do whatever it takes, but don't let them give up without giving it their best shot. It's worth all the effort because it's not that unusual for those not sought out to become the great ones, to everyone's surprise but theirs and those who've always believed in them.

10

Injuries

Finding ways to prevent injuries and taking care of them when they do occur are major areas you should be involved in, areas in which your children will need your help very badly.

Kids do get hurt, and not just in sports such as football, boxing, or hockey. Soccer, baseball, gymnastics, track, and almost any athletic endeavor will have a certain level of danger and potential pain. Many injuries are mishandled; they're not diagnosed or treated quickly enough. Sometimes the proper facilities aren't available or sufficient rest and rehabilitation are neglected. Also, many injuries are preventable with more knowledgeable coaching in stretching, conditioning, and the correct fundamentals of a sport.

When I was twelve, playing Pop Warner football, I injured my left ring finger during a preseason scrimmage. An assistant coach, who obviously knew nothing about medical procedures, took my finger and pulled it hard, thinking he could fix it or something. Well, I suddenly had a dislocated knuckle and bone chips where before I only had a minor injury. The finger did not heal throughout the season. It's still misshapen and makes wearing my Super Bowl ring uncomfortable. (The ring had to be sized to fit over my enlarged knuckle, so it slides all over the place when it rests on the normal-sized area.)

While I'm not trying to frighten you or create an even stronger paranoia that your child is going to get hurt, I am hoping to bring a little realism to your fears and misgivings. There *are* ways to prevent the likelihood of many injuries; steps can be taken to lessen their discomfort, severity, and duration; and experts are available to assist with more serious accidents and their rehabilitation.

ORGANIZING A MEDICAL NETWORK

Questions: Don't you think that young kids need to have good medical attention? High schools, colleges, and professionals have trainers and team doctors. But kids get hurt too. Where can they turn for care, advice, and sound treatment?

Answers: The establishment of a sports medical network for each and every league would vastly improve the safety of youth sports. Kids don't have their own doctors, trainers, or physical therapists, so access to medical information, diagnosis, treatment, and rehabilitation must somehow be found and made available to them. Young athletes who get hurt need immediate, proper care just as much as high school, college, and professional athletes.

Ideally this medical network would be made up of an experienced sports physician, a trainer, and a physical therapist. The services provided by these professionals would be instructional information for parents and coaches covering prevention, handling of on-field injuries and emergencies, access to a hospital, and proper rehabilitation before returning to competition.

How do you go about setting up a network for your league?

First, find a physician. Since you want one who is knowledgeable and experienced in handling sports injuries, go to your local high school or college and find out the name of their team doctor. If this doctor is not available, he or she should be able to direct you to other physicians in the area who have expertise and an interest in sports medicine.

Once a relationship has been arranged, have the doctor come to a meeting of coaches and parents to instruct them on handling injuries during practice or games and the proper positioning for movement and transportation to the hospital as well as life-saving routines. Since the doctor won't be on the sidelines, in most cases, it is important to your child's health that a coach or a parent knows what to do when a player gets hurt. Someone at the site must know what injuries are most serious, how they should be dealt with, and how to diagnose quickly what degree of medical attention is necessary. Some accidents obviously call for immediate professional movement to a hospital while others can be administered to safely on the following day during normal office hours. Make sure the doctor also arranges access to facilities at a hospital, as is done by upper-level team physicians. It is very important that proper attention be readily available.

A trainer can be recruited in much the same fashion as the doctor. He or she should address the same assembly of coaches and parents, and cover such topics as how to tape ankles or jammed fingers and how to prevent and treat sore, strained, or pulled muscles. Concepts such as the importance of having water available at practice, replacing lost salt and minerals, particularly during the hot, humid summer months, and recognizing the signs of heat stroke and exhaustion should be discussed. Also, handling minor on-the-field injuries and basic first aid would fall under the trainer's expertise to be passed on to those who will be on the field in his or her place.

Physical therapists are crucial in rehabilitating injuries, particularly after broken bones and surgeries that have resulted in long layoffs. Returning to competition too soon or without adequate professional guidance can result in unnecessary reinjury as well as new injuries caused by lack of strength, conditioning, or flexibility. The therapist can suggest exercises and running, stretching, and strengthening programs.

Finding and organizing a league's medical network is certainly something the parents, coaches, and a sports-organizing committee should work together to make a reality. It would be helpful, though, if doctors, trainers, and physical therapists would offer their services and those of their colleagues to the local youth groups instead of waiting to be asked for their help.

Tremendous advances have been made in sports medicine. Don't limit their assistance to the much smaller number of athletes at the high school, college, and professional levels. It's unfair to your children, who deserve every advantage possible in their formative years.

SPORTS PHYSICIANS

Questions: Is it really that important for injured athletes to find doctors who specialize in sports medicine instead of just going to any doctor for diagnosis and treatment? And if it is, why?

Answers: I feel it is essential to find a doctor who has a good background in handling athletic injuries. It's great if you can bring your child to a sports medicine clinic where the physicians specialize in the prevention and treatment of sports injuries, but it's not always possible. However, there are many doctors, including medical specialists in fields such as podiatry, hand surgery, and orthopedics, who are interested in sports and treat a great number of athletes as part of their patient work load. Many of these are team doctors or consultants for high schools and colleges.

There are many reasons for finding doctors who have been around sports. First of all, they are experienced in preventing and diagnosing injuries. Many serious medical problems can be avoided by proper early detection and rehabilitation. Remember, many athletes ruin their careers by failing to rest and by not allowing minor injuries to heal. They may hobble around on a sore ankle, ruin a knee, or throw differently when their shoulder hurts, permanently damaging their elbow.

If your child is injured, see a doctor to find out if there are any serious implications. Don't allow the child to play through the pain. Let an experienced medical source advise what to do and how soon it should be done. Too many athletes shrug off injuries or try to diagnose them with no knowledge or medical background; they may end up losing or limiting their future in sports.

If the injury is serious, such as ligament damage in the knee or anything broken, you definitely want a doctor who has handled these injuries and their rehabilitation. Not only will you receive better treatment, such as excellent surgery, but in many cases technological advances and techniques may save a lot of pain and time in recovering. I've known many athletes who have had orthoscopic surgery on knees and elbows and been back within weeks. In fact, Dan Ross, an All-Pro tight end, once had surgery on a Monday and played seven days later on "Monday Night Football." A few years ago he probably would have been in a cast after an operation and out of action for months.

One word of caution, however: Sports medicine is in its infancy, and not all the answers are available. There are many differing opinions on surgical techniques, rehabilitation, and prevention of injuries. Before any decision about continuing play after being hurt or undergoing any kind of surgery is made, I strongly suggest that you get second or third opinions whenever possible. Sometimes surgery is necessary—it certainly saved my career after damaging my shoulder and knee—but many times it can be avoided by rest, supervised strength training, and rehabilitation.

Sports medicine is a growing, evolving field. Besides those doctors who have dedicated themselves to it for the past few decades, there are many young doctors, many trained by the pioneers, who are making athletic injuries a large part of their practice. In seeking out these qualified, experienced physicians, you have a greater chance of finding out what is wrong, what to do about it, and how to prevent its recurrence. Instead of merely treating injuries, these doctors are working to prevent them by developing training programs, using better equipment, and promoting safer playing conditions.

If an injury occurs, find a sports physician. Give your kids every opportunity for the best chance of recovery, a safe return to play, and health after their playing days are over.

PHYSICAL THERAPISTS

Questions: Are physical therapists really that important after you've had surgery? They're expensive and time consuming. If you've had a successful operation, isn't rest and working back into shape enough?

Answers: If a serious injury occurs, a good physical therapist in charge of the rehabilitation is absolutely as important as the surgery itself. No operation, particularly on an athlete, is successful without proper, professionally supervised therapy. There is no question in my mind that I would never have made it through all of my injuries if it hadn't been for my physical therapists, Mike Hairston and Tim Daley. I've watched too many athletes try to rehabilitate themselves or not go consistently to a therapist; their careers were shortened or ended needlessly.

Here are the reasons I strongly believe in the necessity of going with dedication and consistency to an experienced physical therapist after any serious injury, whether or not it entails surgery:

- In many cases, doctors see the patient only a couple of times. Although they might explain the injury and what must be done to rehabilitate it, the terms and information they use may slip by without being understood or be forgotten within a few days by an inexperienced, nervous patient or parent.
- A physical therapist has the tremendous advantage of seeing the patient several times a week over an extended period of time. This allows him or her to explain exactly what is wrong in everyday, simple terms; to answer the questions that inevitably crop up; to outline the method and procedures involved

in the rehabilitation; to motivate the patient; and, by sharing an honest, positive perception of what can be done, eliminating many of the fears and insecurities your child will suffer.

- Therapists are great because they can combine their medical and academic background with experience in the field to make decisions on what course to take in rehabilitation. They become personal consultants to the injury. You have to remember that no two injuries are alike; each is unique and needs to be handled according to its individual needs. The therapist can bypass problems and make corrections that will ultimately save time and energy as well as increase the odds of regaining as much natural use of the injured area as possible.

- Many athletes have surgery or suffer a serious injury of some type, rest a while, and then try to work their way through the pain and get themselves back into shape. This is foolish. A physical therapist will bring an athlete through the various stages of rehabilitation over a safer, more effective time period. From range of motion through strengthening exercises and slowly working back to jogging or throwing, the therapist will oversee and gauge the progress being made. Too many athletes are hurt by stretching too much and too soon or lifting heavy weights or trying to compete at too early a point in rehabilitation.

- Many injuries are never healed, even after successful surgery or rest, because the athletes fail to work hard and intelligently under the guidance of an experienced therapist. Either they lose flexibility, keep reinjuring the area, or never regain the strength they had once possessed.

203

- Although therapists certainly do make errors, they can increase the chances of playing again and regaining the maximum use of the injured area. They're not only valuable as medical experts but as friends who can help your child through the painful and many times frightening experience of rehabilitating a serious injury.

PLAYING HURT VERSUS PLAYING INJURED

Questions: I know that kids shouldn't play when they're injured, but aren't there some injuries they need to learn to handle? You hear about pro athletes playing hurt all the time. I guess it is heroic, but it seems to set a dangerous example for youngsters who feel they have to prove they're tough too. Where do you draw the line?

Answers: Pro players do play when they're hurt but rarely will they play when they're injured—and there's a huge difference between the two. Let me explain.

Playing "hurt" means that although the athlete has a physical problem involving some pain or discomfort, perhaps even limiting his ability to perform at full strength, there is little chance of long-term or permanent damage. Playing "injured" involves playing when there's a great risk of seriously aggravating or compounding an injury.

Many times kids will have little things wrong with them that involve some discomfort but won't stop them from playing. Part of sports is learning to cope with bruises, sore muscles, or maybe even a slightly sprained finger. It'll be no different when they grow up—they'll go to work sometimes when they're not feeling particularly well.

Working when you have a cough or cold is far different from trying to push through pneumonia, however. One is expected, the other is dangerous and a threat to the individual's health. So it should be in athletics. Players have to learn to handle some pain, but they should never, on any level, threaten their health. No game is big enough, no championship is as valuable as even one player's body.

Playing with an injured knee or pulled muscle on the youth level is inexcusable. Kids don't have the ability to make a decision on how far they can push. For them, distinguishing between playing "hurt" and playing "injured" is neither fair nor possible.

There is a huge difference between professional athletes playing in pain and kids trying to do the same. Even the pros have to learn to protect themselves, to know when they're threatening themselves with more serious injury by continuing. Remember, too, that they have trainers to help protect them and treat their injuries, and they have doctors to diagnose and define the injury.

Professional players are more mature. They're more experienced and better equipped to "read" and understand their bodies. But even with the advantages of medical supervision and their own experience as guides, too many pros shorten or ruin their careers by performing when they should be resting and rehabilitating.

Don't allow this to happen to your children. This is a definite case in which playing it safe is playing it smart.

R.I.C.E.
(Rest, Ice, Compression, Elevation)

Have you ever wondered whether it's better to stick a sore thumb or ankle in a hot whirlpool or put ice on it? I frequently ask people what they think the correct answer is and, amazingly, most of them guess heat. Wrong. Heat shouldn't be used for at least two or three days after most injuries. Ice is best, but it's only part of the most often accepted treatment formula commonly referred to as R.I.C.E. (the initials standing for rest, ice, compression, and elevation).

Rest is very important and too often neglected after accidents. Instead of your children risking further injury by running or playing through the pain, get them off their feet and resting immediately.

Begin icing the injured area thoroughly, either submerged in cold water or by using ice packs. Do this for fifteen to twenty minutes several times a day. The ice will shrink the torn blood vessels. This is important because the more blood that collects around the injury, the longer it will take to heal. Do not ice for longer than twenty minutes at any one time because this can actually reverse the results and cause more swelling.

Make sure to wrap or cover the area with a cold, moist compress (a bandage or a towel previously soaked and drained in cold water). This will limit swelling and help speed up the healing process.

Elevating the injured part should be done by placing it above the heart level. Gravity will drain the excess fluid that has collected. If it's an ankle, simply prop it on a few pillows; if it's a hand or arm, the injured player should hold it above the chest as much as possible.

After forty-eight hours or so you can start using heat. This will stimulate blood flow and open up the blood vessels, allowing more nutrients, oxygen, and anti-inflammatory cells to the area. These will all induce quicker healing. To further speed up the process, you can also use contrasts (alternating heat for four minutes with ice for one minute). Repeat this several times and do these sessions four or five times a day. Be sure to always start with heat and finish with cold.

As effective as this treatment is, however, remember that if there is any sharp pain, discoloration, or swelling, your child should see a doctor and get X rays as soon as possible. Let a professional tell you whether your child is injured seriously. There's no place for "playing hurt" in youth sports, so ensure your child's safety whenever there is any doubt.

BLISTERS

Question: Every year when I start playing basketball I get blisters on my feet. I can't seem to get any answers about how to prevent them or what to do once I get them. Should they be opened up or left alone until they heal?

Answer: Any question involving blisters really hits home for me. I've suffered through them for years, unable to figure out how to prevent them and what to do with them. This "minor" injury is painful and can affect your kids' performance if it is not dealt with promptly and properly.

Here are a few things that I've found helpful in preventing or at least lessening the impact of blisters, particularly on the feet. Make sure to wear shoes that fit comfortably. Place some lubrication such as Vaseline on those areas that always seem to cause trouble. Try to condition the feet before heavy play begins by practicing the drills that will put the most stress on the feet.

Treatment and care of blisters is important and can make a great deal of difference. If there is fluid in the blister, it should be removed because studies have shown that a blister heals faster after the fluid is drained. To do this, cleanse the skin surrounding the damaged area with alcohol and then sterilize a needle by heating it over a flame until it turns bright red. After the needle cools, puncture the edge of the blister and press the skin until the fluid drains.

Be sure to leave the skin on top of the blister intact because it will protect the wound from infection and provide a cover until the healing process is well under way. If you cut off the skin, you'll have an open wound that is not only more painful but more likely to become infected. Before practicing or playing, place a small doughnut-shaped pad over the blister or some tape without gauze. Use a surgical soap such as Phisoderm every day to further cleanse the wound and prevent infection.

Finally, try to begin each season with shoes that are well broken in. New shoes almost always guarantee blisters, so wear older, comfortable footwear early in the season and break in new shoes gradually.

BRUISED MUSCLES

Bruised muscles are the most common injuries and almost unavoidable in team sports. Although not serious in most cases, they still hurt and should be taken care of, not just ignored. These involve ruptured blood vessels, so it's important to control swelling. Particularly in large muscle groups such as in the legs, there can be a lot of bleeding;

therefore, icing for three to four days is important to avoid soreness, tightness, and delays in recovery.

The muscles surrounding the injured area should be stretched gently. This will hasten regaining full range of motion and break up the adhesions that have formed and that often inhibit a full return to action. Avoiding reinjury can be tricky since many bruises occur in vulnerable areas, but extra padding can go a long way in protecting your child from continued discomfort.

One serious concern with muscle bruises, particularly in the thigh region, is that they can calcify. If discomfort and pain persist, take your child to a physician to make sure the injury doesn't have more serious complications.

Another bothersome bruise that is all too often ignored is one on the heel. Have you ever stepped on a rock while walking barefoot and felt like screaming out? For an athlete this little scenario can cause major problems. Heel bruises are tough to get rid of in competition. The constant pounding tends to irritate and then worsen what began as a minor condition.

Rest is crucial. A few days off and thorough icing should ensue. After a couple of days begin treatments with moist heat; soak the foot in a whirlpool or tub of hot water for periods of twenty-five minutes, three to four times a day. Make sure your child stays off his or her feet as much has possible to avoid irritating the bruise, then try to find something to comfortably absorb the shock and protect the heel. A heel cup that fits into a shoe or some padding, such as a doughnut-shaped pad, can be effective. Experimenting first while just walking, instead of attempting to go back to full workouts involving running and jumping at full speed, is the way to go.

Don't take your child's bruises too lightly. Mishandling these little injuries can make children wary, cost them the pleasure of competition and, in some extreme cases, lead to unnecessary chronic conditions. Make sure they rest adequately, have time to use the treatments that will speed up recovery, and use any protective pad or equipment that can prevent unnecessary reinjury.

MUSCLE CRAMPS: WHY?

Muscle cramps are problems for six-year-olds all the way to professional athletes. They can be very painful and have to be dealt with on several levels. Every year, particularly in preseason camp and during early season games when it's hot and muggy, many NFL players fall victim to cramps. Kids are no different, and if ignored, cramps can lead to more serious injuries such as muscle strains and pulls.

Make sure your children are getting enough salt (no salt pills, though), magnesium, and potassium in their diet. Fruits (especially bananas), fresh vegetables, and grains are great sources for these minerals. Also, they should drink plenty of liquids before, during, and after every workout.

As soon as cramping begins, exercise should stop. Gentle stretching and massage should follow immediately. You have probably seen trainers doing this to athletes on the sidelines during games on television. But even though those players often go back to play, be careful about allowing your children to return to action unnecessarily.

Many cramps are also caused by overexertion—the muscles are simply tired—so insist that your children work up to higher levels of conditioning instead of overdoing too fast or too often. Allowing muscles to recover with rest and always warming up thoroughly with stretching and jogging before full-speed activity are important too. Coaches should also try to plan workouts when it's cooler, either early in the morning or during the late afternoon in the hot season.

If cramping persists after all these precautions, a doctor should be consulted and an analysis of mineral levels should be done. The doctor will be able to tell you the specific foods needed to replenish the minerals your child's body has lost, which is quite often the cause of recurring problems with cramps.

Muscle Cramps: What to Do

Question: When my child gets cramps, is it all right for him to play through them or should he quit for the day?

Answer: Your child shouldn't try to play through muscle cramps. Instead, your child should go to the sideline and gently stretch the muscle until the spasms stop, then rest and passively stretch the area. Drinking fluids while resting and waiting for the contractions to cease and then beginning warm-ups again with some jogging and stretching are the next steps.

If the child feels better after this, then returning to action cautiously is possible. But be aware that muscle pulls are a real danger when an athlete is fatigued, and if care is not taken, it's possible to sustain a much more serious injury. If severe cramps ever hit, then immediately bring the athlete to a hospital and have the body fluids replenished through intravenous feedings.

Now for a nonmedical tip that seems to help, as taught to me by the Cincinnati Bengals' trainer: When a cramp occurs, have the child pinch his or her upper lip steadily and hard. This sounds weird but can sometimes relieve the pain and allow play to continue. And, yes, although I knew it was pretty strange looking, I've used it many times, and it has worked for me.

MUSCLE PULLS

Muscle pulls are very common and can be very damaging. They are an active tear of muscle or tendon fibers, and their severity is based on the percentage of fibers damaged. There will be a sudden pain that is localized and persistent. If adequate rest and treatment are not immediately employed, pulls can become chronic; the tears can worsen and force inactivity.

Muscle pulls can be caused by a great many factors. The most common is poor warm-ups. Athletes can't go out and start running, jumping, or throwing without stretching and warming up slowly. If they do, they're just asking for pulls. Muscles are stiff and tight, and are without much elasticity until they are gradually loosened through stretching and jogging.

Fatigue also can lead to many pulls. Every year, a few weeks into their training camps, you'll see professional athletes begin to suffer injured hamstrings and groins. These occur in many cases because they've worked hard, their muscles are tight and sore, and they haven't had adequate time to recover through rest, so they strain, pull, or tear them.

Poor flexibility can also lead to these injuries. Make sure your kids stretch before and after all workouts. They should take the time to slowly, gradually stretch and lengthen their muscles. Tight, shortened muscles are much more susceptible to injury, so consistently working on greater flexibility can protect young athletes.

Lack of sodium, potassium, or magnesium can sometimes result in muscle pulls too. Make sure diets include foods that contain these minerals. They must be replaced when lost through perspiration, particularly in hot, humid weather.

Physical problems such as unequal arm or leg length, flat feet, or a curved back can also cause muscle pulls because excess stress may be placed on specific muscles. Occasionally muscle imbalance, in which one muscle is stronger or more flexible than its opposing muscle, can cause the more powerful to damage the weaker. It becomes important, therefore, to stretch both legs equally.

Accelerated or overtraining is another problem area. All athletes should increase their work load gradually, not suddenly go out and put tremendous strain on muscles without adequate conditioning. If the muscles have not been prepared or prove incapable of handling a sudden increase in stress, they will probably be injured.

Finally, make sure some endurance training is included in workouts. Distance running or bicycle riding will thicken muscles, tendons, and ligaments, which then tend to be more resistant to pulls. A year-round program of conditioning, weight lifting, and stretching should be part of athletic preparation as children mature and reach higher levels of competition.

Treating a Muscle Pull

Question: I've pulled a muscle. What is the best way to treat the injury, and what can I do to make sure I don't reinjure it in the future?

Answer: There is a tremendous range in the severity of an injured muscle, from a slight strain, to a pull, to a complete tear. Each injury calls for a different amount of rest, treatment, and rehabilitation. The first thing to do if a muscle is injured is get to an experienced sports physician for diagnosis, medication (if necessary), and a rehabilitation program.

One error I've seen far too many athletes make is trying to return to action too quickly after hurting a muscle. Generally they reinjure the area by coming back too soon and going at full speed without adequate rest and supervised treatment. In many cases this has resulted in ruining their entire season, and the injury has become a chronic problem, contributing to a premature end to their careers.

Muscle injuries are serious matters. After seeing a doctor, make sure to find a trainer and/or physical therapist to guide you through a thorough rehabilitation. During the first forty-eight hours you should use R.I.C.E. (Rest, Ice, Compression, Elevation). Holding down the amount of swelling and bleeding in the muscle can greatly speed up the healing process, so avoid heat, which brings blood into the area.

During the time of recovery it's essential that conditioning the rest of the body is continued. Taking time off does not mean avoiding training all together. Make sure to work the good leg, the upper body, and the arms so that strength and endurance will not be lost.

Walking both forward and backward easily should begin after a couple of days. Performing normal functions like these will gently stretch the muscles and prepare them for the flexibility and strength exercises that will lead to recovery.

For flexibility, begin with the hurdler's stretch and toe touching. The stretching should go only as far as a feeling of tightness; pushing to the point of pain could reinjure or irritate the muscle. The stretches should be smooth, with no bouncing, and last from twenty to thirty seconds. Tearing a muscle tends to shorten it; therefore, it's necessary to relengthen it carefully through stretching.

For strength, start with hamstring curls. Leaning against a wall with arms extended and lifting the leg with an ankle weight or weighted boot serving as resistance is good. It's also effective to use a weight machine that entails lying on a bench and lifting the heel toward the buttocks. In either case the exercises should be performed carefully, using light weights and high repetitions, and stopping when any pain or fatigue is felt.

After strength and flexibility have been regained, walking and then slow jogging should begin. As these become comfortable, move on to controlled striding in a straight line. After this is handled easily, running in large figure eights and gradually making them smaller as the ability to cut increases is an important exercise. Do not hurry through this phase of rehabilitation. Taking extra time and gaining confidence in the leg's ability to perform can prevent unnecessary reinjury and increase the chances of a smooth recovery.

Upon returning to practice, going full speed or getting involved in every drill should be avoided. Instead, an athlete should start with the exercise period and some of the less strenuous parts of the team's workouts. As timing, confidence, and strength return, add drills until it's possible to comfortably perform all of the necessary physical requirements of the sport and of a particular position. Only then should a return to full activity and games be attempted.

Taking the proper steps and using intelligence, patience, and discipline are all necessary to overcome a muscle pull and to regain the strength and flexibility lost through the injury. Hurrying back, cutting corners, or refusing to find and follow proper professional supervision could have disastrous results, most of which can be avoided.

SHINSPLINTS

Shinsplints is a very painful condition and if not treated properly will keep getting worse until the pain prevents an athlete from continuing activity.

The term "shinsplints" is a catch-all that really involves a possibility of four different injuries. The most common is a sprain or rip of the tibial and toe extensor muscles, starting in the back of the lower leg and going to the foot's arch. The second is an inflammation of the covering of the lower leg bone. The two less common injuries are an interruption of the blood flow to the three muscles of the front of the lower leg and stress fractures to the lower leg bone.

It's not enough just to say your child has shinsplints and let it go at that. If the pain continues after trying the treatment that follows, see a doctor and find out specifically what the problem is.

The basic, surest cure is rest and ice. Ice the damaged area for fifteen to twenty minutes, twice daily. Also do gentle, progressive stretching of the calf muscles to help prevent further problems.

Prevention of shinsplints involves many factors. First of all, buy your children good, well-padded pairs of shoes. Then carefully select the surfaces they work out on; they should do their running on dirt or grass, for instance. If they're into aerobics, make sure they avoid doing their workouts on tile, wood, or cement. The flooring should be carpeted and well padded.

Another area to consider is how much they're doing and how prepared their legs are for the work load being placed on them. Cut down on the distance and days they run if they begin feeling pain in their legs. Insist that they work gradually into longer runs and onto tougher terrains.

Warming up is also very important. Make sure your kids

stretch and loosen up before taking off on any run. They should pay particular attention to stretching the calf muscles.

After finishing, make sure they cool down. Walking for a little while and doing some gentle stretches to help cool down their muscles are important. They might also want to ice down their legs as an added precaution.

Shinsplints is a common ailment at every level of athletics, from the overzealous beginner to the occasional weekend overdoer or the professional. Remember, the best medicine is trusting the body. If the legs start hurting, rest should begin immediately; trying to run through the pain will only worsen the condition. If rest doesn't improve the condition, be sure to see a physician.

TENDONITIS

Question: Both of my sons have had problems with their Achilles tendons and have been told they have tendonitis. I play racquetball, and when my shoulder was sore, I was told the same thing. What exactly is tendonitis, and what is the proper treatment?

Answer: Tendonitis is a swelling or inflammation caused by tight muscles. It generally relates to those areas an athlete or anyone uses most commonly and strenuously. For example, in running sports such as football, basketball, track, and soccer, Achilles tendonitis is most common. Likewise, in throwing sports such as tennis, racquetball, and baseball, tendonitis is found most often in the shoulder and wrist.

Tendonitis is one of the most common recurring injuries in sports. It's unique because athletes in the early stages can play through the discomfort, and they therefore often resist getting proper medical attention. Initially there is a dull pain. There is stiffness in the morning, but as the day wears on the injured area loosens up and the pain decreases. In practices or games the pain subsides further, but six to eight hours after competition it intensifies significantly. This cycle continues and the injured area worsens until the athlete is unable to perform because of the pain or until a more serious injury, such as a tendon tear or rupture, occurs.

Most medical authorities agree that rest is the absolute best treatment for any type of tendonitis. Once you've detected the early stages of pain, your child should stop the activity causing it. Ice the area twice daily for a few days, and then begin stretching slowly, but rest from the activity for two weeks. If you take the child to a doctor, he or she may prescribe anti-inflammatory pills to ease the swelling. Pain pills or steroid injections should be taken only with great caution because these can mask the pain, with the result that an athlete can be seriously injured without being aware of it until it's too late.

A cortisone injection, if placed directly in a tendon, can weaken it and lead to a tear or rupture, so be careful about accepting this kind of treatment.

After a couple of weeks of rest there should be a reexamination; if given the okay, the athlete must work to get back into shape slowly. Make sure the oral anti-inflammatory medication the doctor may have prescribed is continued to be taken. Stretching and warming up carefully and as fully as possible should come first, then jogging, throwing, or swinging easily and smoothly before going full speed. Running on softer surfaces, such as cinder tracks or grass fields, also helps prevent much of the pounding and the chances of irritation.

Don't let your kids rush their return. They should take as much rest as necessary and return to the sport when their body tells them it's all right. If pushed too fast, the problem will just recur and may become chronic.

Preventing tendonitis is difficult. Make sure that your children wear proper fitting, well-padded shoes, that they work out on soft surfaces whenever possible, and that they stretch and warm up fully every time they compete. And if they feel pain in a specific area, have them see a doctor and rest instead of trying to work through the pain. They'll be far better off both in the short term and in the long run if they use caution and seek professional guidance immediately.

THUMBS AND FINGERS

Sprained and dislocated fingers and thumbs are common in many sports, particularly football, basketball, and baseball. These injuries, often put aside as troublesome little bothers, should not be overlooked or taken lightly. A young athlete may have suffered a far more serious injury than is at first suspected. A third-degree sprain or a dislocation can lead to lifelong problems such as a chronically unstable finger or thumb. The necessity of corrective surgery may be the price of not having the joint initially diagnosed, treated, and rehabilitated professionally.

If your child hurts a finger or thumb, take him or her to a doctor immediately. The area should be X-rayed to make sure there is no fracture, and the severity of the sprain should be determined. The physician, after deciding whether a splint is necessary, will suggest strengthening and range of motion exercises and explain the proper treatment for the particular injury.

Many athletes, including me, have ignored having injured fingers treated properly, and the results have ranged from ugly, deformed joints to the inability to straighten a finger or arthritis. Don't allow your kids to try to play through the pain with the hope that the problem will go away. If you don't take this injury more seriously, it could lead to a major problem and impair future athletic performance.

Jammed thumbs and fingers are maddening. If not taken care of, they seem to linger forever. Treatment is essential. After icing for two or three days, begin heat treatments.

While soaking the injured part in very warm water three times a day, have your child do some exercises to regain flexibility and range of motion. This should be continued for several days before returning to play. Resting and allowing the swelling to go down are critical in overcoming this type of injury.

Once your child returns to action, taping the injured finger to an adjacent finger for added strength and stability is recommended. Do this by applying the tape to the flat areas above and below the knuckles to allow movement. Continue this for at least two weeks.

I know that kids don't want to miss any action, but unless you have finger injuries diagnosed and treated properly right away, they will persist, worsen, and perhaps ruin an entire season. You'll probably find that in the long run an athlete is far better off taking the time to rest and protect the finger or thumb under medical supervision.

THE ANKLE

Sprained ankles should never be taken lightly. The days of walking them off and continuing to play through the pain and risking greater injury should end. The swelling of an ankle or any joint is an indication that medical attention and immediate rest are required.

Have your child go to a physician and have X rays taken to make sure there are no fractures or bone chips. At that time the doctor can also determine the severity of damage, if any, to ligaments, tendons, or muscles, and outline the best combination of rest and treatment.

Do not apply heat such as whirlpools or warm baths to sprained ankles for at least forty-eight hours. Go with ice, a compression (a wrap around the area), and elevation to keep down the swelling. After two or three days of rest and ice, begin contrasting heat and cold. Place the ankle in very warm water for four minutes and then cold for one. Repeat this with a little cautious walking in between every day. Also, while the foot is submerged, move the ankle gently in different directions to regain flexibility and range of motion.

Don't be surprised if the ankle continues hurting for a while, but make sure that prior to returning to full-speed competition the injured athlete takes enough time to work back into shape and uses extra means of protection. The ankle should be taped, and the athlete should begin with walking, then straight-ahead jogging, followed by easy figure eights for slow, easy cutting and direction changes, then half-speed practice before full play.

Ankle injuries can become chronic problems if not handled properly. Also, knee injuries can result from the unnatural running motion an athlete may adopt to compensate for the injured leg.

Don't allow this to happen and then blame a coach. It's the parents' responsibility to look out for their children's health. In the future you can protect them from overzealous, uninformed coaches as well as from themselves by insisting that they receive immediate professional medical diagnosis, sound treatment and, finally, intelligent rehabilitation before they take the field again.

Too many athletes have recurring ankle problems because they've never rested, rehabilitated, and *strengthened* the injured ligaments or tendons properly. In many instances they go back into full competition too quickly and reinjure themselves unnecessarily. Although taping and wraps do supply some additional support, they cannot substitute for strong, healthy ankles.

The key is to use ankle supports when in full, highly competitive situations but to work carefully and diligently on strengthening the ankles outside of these activities. Weight lifting such as toe raises on the leg press machine and controlled running and cutting without support can help to protect and improve a young athlete's ankle problems.

With cleats, grass, uneven surfaces, and all of the sharp cuts and moves that are so much a part of sports, ankle injuries are very common in all athletics. Many players are fortunate enough to avoid them, but precautions are important and necessary for some. But don't camouflage the problem by turning to taping with the hope that the injury will go away. Go to a physical therapist, get some exercises, and have your child work long and hard to strengthen and protect the ankle. Taping should be used as an extra measure to prevent injury, not as a long-range corrective treatment.

SHOULDERS

I have had both a shoulder separation and a torn rotator cuff. Not only are these injuries painful but rehabilitating them involves discipline, dedication, and intelligent supervision by an experienced physical therapist.

Work should begin as soon as possible after the injury. It's important to continue exercising the other muscle groups not involved with the shoulder. Running with the shoulder in a sling will cut down on the motion and jarring of the area and will keep the cardiovascular foundation and leg strength intact. If running hurts too much, then using a stationary bicycle will substitute satisfactorily. Also, working the good arm with some weight lifting without affecting the separated shoulder is beneficial.

It's crucial to regain as much strength and range of motion as possible during rehabilitation. Lifting weights and some isometric exercises will strengthen the muscles in the shoulder and tighten the joint. Doing stretching and resistance movements will also help, but be sure to work on strength and flexibility equally. One without the other negates the gains that have been made.

Your therapist may suggest the Codman's exercises for range of motion, named for the physician who developed them. These include allowing the arm to hang down and moving it in clockwise and then counterclockwise circles starting with small rotations and working up to larger circles; also, moving the arm slowly up from your side as high as possible and walking your fingers up a wall for reach and extension. For strength, good exercises are bicep curls and tricep extensions, using either dumbbells or machines designed for this purpose, and lateral pull-downs with the hands placed close together on the bar. External rotation is important, and a good exercise for this is lying on your good side with the injured arm against that side, bent at the elbow at a ninety-degree angle. Then slowly move the weight back and forth without the elbow leaving the side. This will strengthen the muscle surrounding the rotator cuff. Another good exercise is bench pressing on a machine (not free weights) where the bar has been adjusted higher than the ordinary starting position, thus allowing for a mechanical advantage and eliminating the part of the lift that would be most dangerous to this injury.

It's important to push intelligently through the recovery. Avoiding pain and any activity that could result in another dislocation is obviously of foremost concern. Steer clear of anything involving a throwing motion since this places great stress on the joint.

Unfortunately, once a shoulder has been separated the chances of recurrence are 50 percent higher than someone who has never had this injury, and the odds keep going up each time the joint is reinjured. However, many athletes return to action after a thorough rehabilitation and suffer no further problems. Luck is always a factor, but the best form of protection is strengthening the muscles in the shoulder area and reclaiming as much flexibility as possible before returning to competition.

If the problem becomes chronic, avoid any activity that presents a threat, even if it means giving up a favorite sport. The pain and risks to are simply too high.

THE NECK

Question: Our son will be playing football this year on the varsity level in high school. We are very frightened by the number of neck injuries players suffer in this sport. Are there ways to minimize the chances of neck injuries and protect against them happening?

Answer: Unfortunately, because football is a contact sport, neck injuries are more common than in most other athletic activities. In blocking, tackling, or even hitting the ground, tremendous force is absorbed by the neck and head. If the neck is hyperextended or hyperflexed, an injury may result. It cannot be stressed enough that *any damage done to* *the neck is serious and should be diagnosed and treated professionally immediately.* Sensations of burning, numbness, loss of strength, headaches, and nausea are all warning signs that medical attention is necessary.

Protecting the neck while playing football involves two key areas. First, players should be taught proper hitting techniques, the foremost being never to use their helmet as a weapon. Spearing and using the head for impact should not only be outlawed but enforced and severely penalized. Second, good stretching and strengthening programs for the neck should be part of your children's conditioning and training. They should perform these exercises year round, not just seasonally. If they don't have access to neck exercise machines, then they should be doing manual resistance exercises.

While weight training has helped to prevent injuries and has decreased the severity of those that do occur, for some reason strengthening the neck is an area that has not been given enough time and effort. Even those coaches who do stress its importance often neglect to make sure the program is continued during the season. It should be obvious that a football player needs as much protection as possible when he's hitting and being hit. He should faithfully work his neck muscles at least twice a week even when he's sore and tired.

Two rules every coach should enforce are that the neck should be stretched prior to practices and games and, for greatest safety, exercised only after a workout. (Remember, I'm talking about two separate actions: stretching the neck as opposed to exercising the neck.) The stretching will warm up and loosen the muscles to give them greater pliability and flexibility, and will help to prevent injuries. On the other hand, training or strengthening exercises prior to competitions will only tire the muscles and leave the neck fatigued, thus weakened and consequently more susceptible to injury. Again, STRETCH THE NECK BEFORE WORKOUTS AND EXERCISE IT ONLY AFTER WORKOUTS.

If at all possible, make arrangements for your kids to have access to neck strengthening machines such as those built by Nautilus. These provide exercises that will strengthen the neck in all four primary movements: flexibility, extension, lateral bending, and rotation. If a high school doesn't have these machines, perhaps you can get a membership in a health spa or into a college weight room that has them.

If weight machines are unavailable, make sure they begin doing some manual resistance exercises. These are performed with a partner or spotter and require no equipment. One example is the neck extension exercise. In this, the spotter (a teammate, friend, or parent) kneels next to the lifter, who is down on all fours, and places one hand on the back of the lifter's head and the other on his upper back. The lifter lowers the head until the chin touches the chest and then slowly, gradually, raises the head while the spotter applies constant pressure throughout the full range of motion. After a brief pause at the top, the lifter lowers the head against the spotter's pressure until he or she reaches his or her chest. Each repetition should take four or five seconds and be repeated ten to twelve times during each workout. The lifter should constantly be telling the spotter whether the pressure being applied is appropriate.

A serious concern for a child's neck while playing football is fully justified. Now, with research and the development of the exercise machines, the chances of preventing injuries have been greatly increased. I must stress again, however, that you should do whatever it takes to get your athlete on the neck machines.

CONCUSSIONS

Questions: What exactly is a concussion? Once you have one, are you likely to have more? And can I keep playing sports such as football and baseball when I get older?

Answers: Concussions are scary. I can understand fear and concern over them because I've had five myself. Mine came from falling off a fence onto a sidewalk, being slugged twice by ornery linebackers, and twice being "clotheslined" by unfriendly defensive backs. A concussion is actually a mild bruising of brain tissue. Even though the skull is quite hard, a good knock from a tackle in football, an errant baseball, a kick in soccer, or just landing off balance on the head can cause one. Normally your kids won't lose consciousness, but they'll feel woozy and unsure of their feet. In most cases they'll still know who they are, where they are, and what day it is.

After any head injury, make sure to have a doctor check the injured athlete as soon as possible to determine that a much more serious injury such as a skull fracture or an epidural hematoma hasn't been received. These are extremely dangerous, so it's vital to get an immediate, complete examination.

As far as playing when you're older, there should be no problem in competing in football or baseball. Just make sure to wear good helmets in most sports and not to use your head as a battering ram on the gridiron. Tackles should be made with the shoulders, and *never* spear anyone.

KNEES

I think knee injuries scare parents more than any other injury their children can suffer. I've received so many letters and pleas, asking why more can't be done to prevent their occurrence. With all of the advances in weight training, conditioning equipment, and sports medicine, it doesn't seem logical to many moms and dads that these injuries keep destroying careers and threatening the long-term mobility and health of so many athletes.

Unfortunately, particularly in football and basketball, it is impossible to eliminate torn cartilage, stretched and torn ligaments and tendons, and damaged nerves. These sports involve too much contact and stress, and are played on surfaces that invite both instantaneous as well as gradual damage to the knees. Every athlete who participates is at risk, and many factors are involved in avoiding an injury, not the least of which is pure luck.

The good news is that some advances have been made to prevent knee injuries. Many players are now wearing braces as protection. These lightweight devices don't inhibit range of motion or performance, and are easily obtained and relatively inexpensive. Over the past few seasons I have seen several players on the Bengals walk to the sidelines carrying mangled braces in their hands that could have represented damage to their own ligaments if they hadn't been wearing their protective gear. Although conclusive evidence has not been established, knee braces do exemplify one step toward finding effective protection for the knees.

Another factor, which many question, is the apparent ineffectiveness of recent advances in training and sports medicine. There's absolutely no doubt that good weight-lifting and stretching programs combined with solid aerobic and anaerobic training can help an athlete's knees to absorb many of the collisions, unusual body positions, and the wear and tear of years of competition. Besides the added strength and flexibility, conditioning is immensely important because athletes are much more susceptible to injury when they are tired. Fatigue leads to physical and mental error, weakness and, ultimately, a greater likelihood of being hurt. The knees are particularly vulnerable because of their importance in starting and stopping, cutting, and sudden movement, all crucial in so many sports.

Sports medicine is providing ever-improving corrective and preventive answers to knee problems. Advances in arthroscopic surgery have allowed doctors to make more accurate diagnoses by actually probing with a miniature camera within the knee, making only a small incision, then being able to study the film to determine the best solutions. Also, minor repairs and removal of cartilage can be performed, and in many cases the athlete may return to action within a few days. Previously the layoff might have been weeks or even months because of the necessity of immobilization and the healing of the large, painful incision.

There are no guarantees that your children won't face knee surgery someday if they continue in their sports. Although it is possible to cut down the chances, the reality is that a great many athletes do incur damage to their knees. What is somewhat reassuring is the ever-increasing number who are able to return to action and still excel.

Warming Up Sore Knees

Question: I play basketball, and my knees always hurt when I first start playing. I also have a tough time jumping high. Are there any exercises or things I can do to help warm up?

Answer: Through the years I've had many problems with my knees not wanting to do what I demanded of them at the beginning of workouts. Every time I went to play football, basketball, or volleyball they would hurt, and I couldn't really jump until halfway through the first game or well into a practice.

This past year, however, I finally figured out some ways to help avoid both the pain and the temporary loss of jumping ability. First of all, I start by taking a ten-minute whirlpool or hot bath about half an hour before competing. This warms the joints, stimulates circulation, and loosens the muscles, particularly the hamstrings, which are so critical to leaping.

Upon leaving the tub I rub some heat balm all over the affected area and immediately put some sweat pants on, even if it's warm outside.

Once I arrive at the tournament or workout, I stretch a little more and slowly jog at least a half mile. When I get back I start stretching and warming up in earnest, beginning with the first exercise in my Tae Kwon Do training. This entails putting your knees together while standing up, bending down slightly with the hands on the knees, and rotating both knees in full circles, clockwise fifteen to twenty times and then counterclockwise until the joints are loose.

I then go through a full routine of calf, back, hamstring, groin, side, and stomach stretches. After these are finished I again jog for a few minutes and begin little jumps. It's important to progress from light jumps through degrees of exertion before pushing your knees to a total leaping effort.

If it's warm and I feel good enough, I remove my sweats a few minutes prior to playing. I find that not only are my knees feeling better but I can perform at full speed as soon as I need to. This is far better than wasting time getting through the warm-up stages during play, which has cost me innumerable points and victories in the past.

There's one other critical element to this program, and it comes into play after a game or practice is over. I had to learn the discipline of cooling down and icing my knees every single day. You can't just leave the court or field, hop in the shower, and go home. An athlete has to stretch and jog a little after a workout and then apply ice or sit in a cold whirlpool. Not sometimes but every time. Even if he or she is feeling good, it should be done for preventive reasons.

If your children follow this routine, their problems may well cease affecting their play. The most difficult thing will be applying themselves consistently throughout the entire program. Allowing extra time for their own personal warm-ups, not just showing up a few minutes before practice and trying to go full speed, is also critical. Doing the right things after exercising, even if it means being the last to leave the locker room or playing field, will prove well worth the effort.

Conclusion
♦

It's obvious that there will be many physical demands, mental tests, and uncontrollable factors involved in your children's quest for athletic success and enjoyment. I can't emphasize enough that those athletes who have interested, informed, and involved parents have the greatest chance not only for better performance and safety on the field but also for personal development away from competition.

Although talent, dedication, and luck will play major roles in determining your boys' and girls' ultimate performance, health, and competitiveness, it's patience, perspective, and perseverance that may be even more influential. These are elements you must possess and pass on to your kids. You'll have to literally fight through and think through many difficult, emotional situations where your insight can make a tremendous difference.

How many times have you seen a really talented boy or girl suddenly quit a sport? Maybe they're burned out or not doing as well as they should, maybe they're second string. How many kids get turned off from a sport at the youth level because they're a little behind their teammates or can't handle the pressure to perform well?

AS YOUR CHILDREN CLIMB THROUGH THE VARIOUS LEVELS OF COMPETITION, THEY WILL NEED SOMEONE TO GUIDE AND SUPPORT THEM, PARTICULARLY DURING THE TRYING TIMES. THAT SOMEONE SHOULD BE YOU.

Be honest with your children. There will be moments when all the work seems worthless and things happen that don't make sense or won't seem fair, and they might not be. There will be personality conflicts with coaches and losses in which crucial mistakes are made. Injuries and more talented teammates might lead to little play or success.

All of these and many more problems will befall any athlete in organized sports. And when they do, there's no one better than a parent to sit down with and discuss the frustrations and pain.

Often there will be difficult situations to deal with. Remember, very few always get the opportunities they should, athletes included. And no matter how well prepared or deserving, people don't always reach the goals they set for themselves.

Whether an athlete is six years old or a senior in high school, he or she will sometimes encounter frustration and need someone to pull them aside to just talk. As I've said, I can't count the number of times my parents convinced me not to quit. Even when I was playing on the professional level, their support helped keep me going.

It's taken me a long time to figure out that what was important to my parents wasn't just their going to games or practicing with me but their belief in me and desire for my personal development. And, in reality, isn't this a big part of what sports are all about?

SATISFYING YOUR DRIVE TO GIVE YOUR CHIDLREN THE BEST OF EVERYTHING IS AN ONGOING EFFORT AND PROCESS. I hope you'll view this book not only as an aid in protecting your kids from injuries, poor coaching, and their own need to succeed, as well as providing practical tips on improved performance and intelligent use of time, but also, and most important, as a resource. Perspective is very difficult to maintain; emotional decisions will pop up and answers can be tough to come up with when you'll need them most. So I'm hoping you won't throw this volume in some box or bury it in a closet or cabinet. Instead, look up information when you're confused or need direction. I know I haven't covered all the questions you'll confront or provided definitive answers to all the countless problems you'll be forced to face. But perhaps you'll react differently, alter an unhealthy approach, handle a coach or one of your children's dilemmas better by being more fully prepared. You might also come up with different answers, customized for your son or daughter through better knowledge, more experience, and love because you've taken the time to think about the difficulties inherent in our youth sports system.

You can be your children's most valuable asset and you can create and nurture lifelong relationships through their involvement in sports. It truly is up to you, so don't pass on your responsibility to coaches or distance yourself because you have little athletic prowess or experience. Rather, do what any successful parent does: Throw yourself as fully as possible into anything your kids are involved in and give them every advantage and every means of protection you can provide.

Index

♦

235

INDEX